# White Clouds, Green Mountains

**Ruskin Bond** has been writing for over sixty years, and now has over 120 titles in print—novels, collections of short stories, poetry, essays, anthologies and books for children. His first novel, *The Room on the Roof*, received the prestigious John Llewellyn Rhys Award in 1957. He has also received the Padma Shri (1999), the Padma Bhushan (2014) and two awards from Sahitya Akademi—one for his short stories and another for his writings for children. In 2012, the Delhi government gave him its Lifetime Achievement Award.

Born in 1934, Ruskin Bond grew up in Jamnagar, Shimla, New Delhi and Dehradun. Apart from three years in the UK, he has spent all his life in India, and now lives in Mussoorie with his adopted family.

# RUSKIN BOND

## White Clouds, Green Mountains

RUPA

Published by
Rupa Publications India Pvt. Ltd 2016
7/16, Ansari Road, Daryaganj
New Delhi 110002

*Sales centres:*
Allahabad Bengaluru Chennai
Hyderabad Jaipur Kathmandu
Kolkata Mumbai

This is a work of fiction. Names, characters, places and incidents
are either the product of the author's imagination or are used fictitiously
and any resemblance to any actual person, living or dead, events or
locales is entirely coincidental.

ISBN: 978-81-291-4233-7

First impression 2016

10 9 8 7 6 5 4 3 2 1

The moral right of the author has been asserted.

# Contents

# Introduction

I came to live in the mountains almost three decades back. I had been working as a writer and journalist in the cities and towns in the plains. Recently returned from England where I had gone in my late teenage years, I was sure that all I wanted to do was write. I lived in the cities of north India, particularly Delhi, but something was always amiss. When I was a boy, I had spent some years in the Doon valley and in school in Simla. And now, as a man, I found I was increasingly drawn back to life in the mountains.

I finally moved to Mussoorie and became a writer by profession. The mountains that were rooted, unmoving and only slowly changing, welcomed me as though I was now truly back home. For one who had drifted a fair bit they were the anchors who allowed me to set down roots, find my home, a family and also my writing voice. Here, away from the commotion and dust of the plains, in the company of great trees, birds, the fogs, the long winding walks, I was able to imagine ever new places, people and stories.

Yet no one should imagine that life in the mountains is devoid of drama. The pace may be slower here, and the priorities a bit different, but there is no dearth of the stories that one can unearth here. Take for example, my numerous visitors from the forests. There was once a bat who had adopted, what seemed to me, an odd style of flying. Like a dive bomber it flew into my room after dark, looking for tasty moths to snap up. I wondered what was wrong with it, till I found that this indeed was a kind of bat that had been written about earlier—much earlier, in 1884. It pleased me that something that was rare even then had chosen to present itself into my home. Other times, I've had squirrels and praying mantis and birds of various kinds sit at the window or sometimes drop in, take a look and then go their way. We take a good close look at each other when we meet, and I flatter myself to think that perhaps they like what they see—as much as I like having these little guests.

Over these years I have also traipsed a fair bit around these hills and mountains, exploring forests and foothills and hamlets. Some of them have been to the holy spots that dot the high reaches—Kedarnath, Badrinath, Gangotri. Here, the sight of the dramatic sceneries and the high majestic peaks remain etched in the mind long after one has returned home. The moment, in Badrinath, when I opened my eyes one morning and looked out of the window to see the magnificent Nilkantha peak bathed in the light of the rising sun is as astonishing and spectacular in my mind's eye even now.

Living among the mountains also means that I get a front row seat when nature decides to put up some of her more spectacular productions. There have been storms that have blown away the roof or mist that has creeped up and engulfed us all leaving us as white shrouded vague shapes. The trees that grow by my window provide their own daily drama. There are the langurs that leap from the walnut tree right outside the window on to the roof and make so much noise that the birds are frightened away. But it's not just langurs, I have also found little boys and on occasion a sprightly granny who have climbed these trees for the fruits. I feel that these trees can do with a reassuring touch now and then from a friendly neighbour, and when I walk among them I make sure I acknowledge their great and stately presence gratefully.

Now, when I go down to Dehra Dun, the crowds and the traffic, the press of people and the commotion make the town nothing like what it was when I was a boy. But there are some things that still remain. There is the old tamarind tree that stood next to the bank where my grandmother kept her money. The tree still stands, a familiar and comforting presence. For now, the sight of the river in the valley is the same, though I wonder when it might decide to change course or even worse, dry up. And all around the valley remain the green mountains. The mangoes and banyans of the foothills give way to oaks and pines and deodars as the eyes travel up. And finally my eyes rest on the white clouds in the sky above. They will remain as well, even as life changes in the land far below them.

Ruskin Bond

# Mother Hill

It is hard to realize that I've been here all these years—twenty-five summers, winters and Himalayan springs. When I look back to the time of my first coming here, it does seem like yesterday.

That probably sums it all up. Time passes, and yet it doesn't pass; people come and go, the mountains remain. Mountains are permanent things. They are stubborn, they refuse to move. You can blast holes out of them for their mineral wealth, strip them of their trees and foliage, or dam their streams and divert their currents. You can make tunnels and roads and bridges; but no matter how hard they try, humans cannot actually get rid of the mountains. That's what I like about them; they are here to stay.

I like to think that I have become a part of these mountains, this particular range, and that by living here for so long, I am able to claim a relationship with the trees, wild flowers, and even the rocks that are an integral part of it.

Yesterday at twilight, when I passed beneath a canopy of oak leaves, I felt that I was a part of the forest. I put out my hand and touched the bark of an old tree, and as I turned away, its leaves brushed against my face as if to acknowledge me.

One day, I thought, if we trouble these great creatures too much, and hack away at them and destroy their young, they will simply uproot themselves and march away, whole forests on the move, over the next range and next, far from the haunts of man. I have seen many forests and green places dwindle and disappear. Now there is an outcry. It is suddenly fashionable to be an environmentalist. That's all right. Perhaps, it is not too late to save the little that is left.

By and large, writers have to stay in the plains to make a living. Hill people have their work cut out trying to wrest a livelihood from their thin, calcinated soil. And as for mountaineers, they climb their peaks and move on in search of other peaks.

But to me, as a writer, mountains have been kind. They were kind from the beginning, when I left a job in Delhi and rented a small cottage on the outskirts of the hill station. Today, most hill stations are rich men's playgrounds, but years ago they were places where people of modest means would live quite cheaply. There were few cars and everyone walked about.

The cottage was on the edge of an oak and maple forest and I spent eight or nine years in it, most of them happy, writing stories, essays, poems and books for children. I think this had something to do with Prem's children. He and his wife had taken on the job of looking after the house and all practical matters (I remain helpless with fuses, clogged cisterns, leaking gas cylinders, ruptured water pipes, tin roofs that blow away when there is a storm, and the do-it-yourself world of small-town India).

Naturally, I grew attached to them and became a part of the family, an adopted grandfather. For Rakesh, I wrote a story about a cherry tree that had difficulty in growing up. For Mukesh, who liked upheavals, I wrote a story about an earthquake and put him in it, and for Dolly I wrote rhymes.

'Who goes to the Hills, goes to his Mother', wrote Kipling, and he seldom wrote truer words. For living in the hills was like living in the bosom of a strong, sometimes proud, but always a comforting mother. And every time I went away, the homecoming would be tender and precious. It became increasingly difficult for me to go away.

It has not always been happiness and light though. There were times when money ran out. Editorial doors sometimes close; but when one door closes another has, for me, almost immediately, miraculously opened.

When you have received love from people and the freedom that only mountains can give, then you have come very near the borders of Heaven.

# Song of the Whistling Thrush

I had been in the hills for a few days when I heard the song of the Himalayan whistling thrush. I did not see the bird that day. It kept to the deep shadows of the ravine below the old stone cottage. I was sitting at the window, gazing out at the new leaves on the walnut and wild pear trees. All was still; the wind was at peace with itself, the mountains brooded massively under the darkening sky. Then, emerging from the depths of the forest like a dark, sweet secret, came the indescribably beautiful call of the whistling thrush.

It is a song that never fails to thrill me. The bird starts with a hesitant schoolboy whistle, as though trying out the melody; then, confident of the time, it bursts into full song, a crescendo of sweet notes and variations that ring clearly across the hillside. Then suddenly the song breaks off, right in the middle of a cadenza, and the enchanted listener is left wondering what happened to the bird to make it stop so suddenly. Nothing really, because a few moments later the song is taken up again.

At first the bird was heard but never seen. Then one day I found the whistling thrush perched on the garden fence. He was a deep, glistening purple, his shoulders flecked with white; he had sturdy black legs and a strong yellow beak; rather a dapper fellow, who could have looked well in a top hat dancing with Fred Astaire. When he saw me coming down the path he uttered a sharp kree-ee—unexpectedly harsh when one remembered his singing—and flew away into the shadowed ravine.

But as the months passed he grew used to my presence and became less shy. One of my rainwater pipes had blocked, resulting in an overflow and a small permanent puddle under the stone steps. This became the thrush's favourite bathing place. On sultry summer afternoons, while I was taking a siesta upstairs, I would hear the bird flapping about in the rainwater pool. A little later, refreshed and sunning himself on the tin roof, he would treat me to a little concert, performed, I cannot help feeling, especially for my benefit.

It was Prakash, the man who brought my milk, who told me the story of the whistling thrush, or the Irstura or Kaljit, as the hillmen called the bird. According to legend, the god Krishna fell asleep near a mountain stream, and while he slept, a small boy made off with his famous flute. On waking up and finding his flute gone, Krishna was so angry that he changed the culprit into a bird; but the boy had played on the flute and learned some of Krishna's wonderful music, and even as a bird he continued, in his disrespectful fashion, to whistle the music of the gods, only stopping now and then (as the whistling thrush does) when he couldn't remember the right time.

It wasn't long before my thrush was joined by a female,

who was exactly like him (in fact, I have never been able to tell one from the other). The pair did not sing duets, like Nelson Eddy and Jeanette MacDonald,* but preferred to give solo performances, waiting for each other to finish before bursting into song. When, as sometimes happened, they started off together, the effect was not so pleasing to my human ear.

These were love calls, no doubt, and it wasn't long before the pair were making forays into the rocky ledges of the ravine, looking for a suitable nesting site; but a couple of years were to pass before I saw any of their young.

After almost two years in the hills, I came to realise that these were birds 'for all seasons'. They were liveliest in midsummer, but even in the depths of winter, with snow lying on the ground, they would suddenly start singing as they flitted from pine to oak to naked chestnut.

As I write, there is a strong wind rushing through the trees and bustling in the chimney, while distant thunder threatens a summer storm. Undismayed, the whistling thrushes are calling to each other as they roam the wind-threshed forest.

At other times I have heard them clearly above the sound of rushing water. And sometimes they leave the vicinity of the cottage and fly down to the stream, half a mile away, sending me little messages on the wind. Down there, they are busy snapping up snails and insects, the chief items on their menu.

Whistling thrushes usually nest on rocky ledges, near water, but my overtures of friendship may have given my visitors other ideas. Recently I was away from Mussoorie for about a fortnight.

---

*Famous singers from my boyhood.

When I returned I was about to open the window when I noticed a large bundle of ferns, lichen, grass, mud and moss balanced outside on the window ledge. Peering through the glass, I was able to recognise this untidy basket as a nest. Could such tidy birds make such untidy nests? Indeed they could, because they arrived and proved their ownership a few minutes later.

Well, of course that meant I couldn't open the window any more—the nest would have gone over the ledge if I had. Fortunately, the room has another window and I kept this one open to let in sunshine, fresh air, and the music of birds, cicadas, and the ever welcome postman.

And now, three pink, freckled eggs lie in the cup of moss that forms the nursery in this jumble of a nest. The parent birds, both male and female, come and go, bustling about very efficiently, fully prepared for the great day that's coming about a fortnight hence.

One small thought occurs to me. The song of one thrush was bright and cheerful. The song of two thrushes was loud and joyful. But won't a choir of five whistling thrushes be a little too much for a solitary writer trying to concentrate at his typewriter? Will I have to make a choice between writing or listening to the birds? Will I have to hand the cottage to other denizens of the forest? Well, we shall have to wait and see. If readers do not hear from me again, they will know who to blame!

# Visitors from the Forest

When mist fills the Himalayan valleys, and heavy monsoon rain sweeps across the hills, it is natural for wild creatures to seek shelter. And sometimes my cottage in the forest is the most convenient refuge.

There is no doubt I make things easier for all concerned by leaving most of my windows open. I like plenty of fresh air indoors, and if a few birds, beasts and insects come in too, they're welcome, provided they don't make too much of a nuisance of themselves.

I must confess, I did lose patience with a bamboo beetle who blundered in the other night and fell into the water jug. I rescued him and pushed him out of the window. A few seconds later he came whirring in again, and with unerring accuracy landed with a plop in the same jug. I fished him out once more and offered him the freedom of the night. But attracted no doubt by the light and warmth of my small sitting-room, he came buzzing back, circling the room like a helicopter looking for a place to land. Quickly I covered the water jug. He landed in a bowl of wild dahlias, and I allowed him to remain there, comfortably curled up in the hollow of a flower.

Sometimes during the day a bird visits me—a deep blue whistling thrush, hopping about on long, dainty legs, too nervous to sing. She perches on the window sill, looking out at the rain. She does not permit any familiarity. But if I sit quietly in my chair she will sit quietly on my window sill, glancing quickly at me now and then to make sure I am keeping my distance. When the rain stops, she glides away, and it is only then, confident in her freedom, that she bursts into full-throated song, her broken but haunting melody echoing down the ravine.

A squirrel comes sometimes, when his home in the oak tree gets water-logged. Apparently he is a bachelor; anyway, he lives alone. He knows me well, this squirrel, and is bold enough to climb on to the dining table looking for titbits which he always finds because I leave them there deliberately. Had I met him when he was a youngster, he would have learnt to eat from my hand; but I have only been here for a few months. I like it this way. I am not looking for pets; these are simply guests.

Last week, as I was sitting down at my desk to write a long-deferred article, I was startled to see an emerald-green praying mantis sitting on my writing-pad. He peered at me with his protuberant glass-bead eyes, and I stared down at him through my glasses. When I gave him a prod, he moved off in a leisurely way. Later, I found him examining the binding of Leaves of Grass; perhaps he had found a succulent bookworm. He disappeared for a couple of days, and then I found him on my dressing-table, preening himself before the mirror.

Out in the garden, I spotted another mantis, perched on the jasmine bush. Its arms were raised like a boxer's. Perhaps they are a pair, I thought, and went indoors, fetched my mantis and placed him on the jasmine bush opposite his fellow insect. He did not like what he saw—no comparison with his own image!—and made off in a hurry.

My most interesting visitor comes at night, when the lights are still burning—a tiny bat who prefers to fly in through the open door, and will use the window only if there is no alternative. His object is to snap up the moths who cluster round the lamps.

All the bats I have seen fly fairly high, keeping near the ceiling; but this particular bat flies in low like a dive bomber, zooming in and out of chair legs and under tables. Once he passed straight between my legs. Has his radar gone wrong, I wondered, or is he just plain mad?

I went to my shelves of natural history and looked up bats, but could find no explanation for this erratic behaviour. As a last resort I turned to an ancient volume, Sterndale's Indian Mammalia (Calcutta, 1884), and in it, to my delight, found what I was looking for: 'A bat found near Mussoorie by Captain Hutton, on the southern range of hills at 1,800 metres; head and body about three centimetres, skims close to the ground, instead of flying high as bats generally do. Habitat, Jharipani, north-west Himalayas.' Apparently, the bat was rare even in 1884.

Perhaps I have come across one of the few surviving members of the species. Jharipani is only three kilometres from where I live. I am happy that this bat survives in my small corner of the woods, and I undertake to celebrate it in prose and verse. Once, I found it suspended upside down from the railing at the foot of my bed. I decided to leave it there. For a writer alone in the woods, even an eccentric bat is welcome company.

# Monkey on the Roof

Quite often, I'm up with the lark; more often, with the sound of monkeys jumping on my tin roof. I've often wondered why hill-station houses must have these rusty red tin roofs, apart from an understandable human desire to make them look like battered old biscuit tins. Well, now I know they are there for the benefit of monkeys, langurs, field-rats, cats, crows, mynas, spiders and scorpions.

I don't mind the spiders, they seem harmless enough. The scorpions are evil-looking but sluggish, unlike the dashing red scorpions of the Rajasthan desert. The other day I found a scorpion enjoying a nap on my pillow. I like to have my pillow to myself, so I tipped the slumbering creature out of the window and returned to my afternoon siesta. I do not take the lives of fellow creatures if I can help it. Cats are not so squeamish. At night they get between the tin roof and the wooden ceiling and create havoc among the rats and mice who dwell there. And early morning, if I leave a window open, the monkeys will finish anything they find on the breakfast table.

In spite of occasional rude awakenings, I enjoy sleeping late, especially on winter mornings when the sun struggles to penetrate banks of cloud or mist or drizzle. The bed is one of my favourite places. And even if I am wide awake, I can be there under the blanket and razai and enjoy the view without rising. The window in front of me looks out on the clouds or the clear sky; the window beside it gives me a view of upper Landour and the houses on the slopes; and the far window looks out on a thicket of oak trees. And if I sit up in bed, I can see the road and some of the people on it.

But to start with my bed, for that's where the day begins and ends. There's something to be said for beds. After all, we spend roughly half our lives stretched out upon them. The amount of time spent in sleep varies from one individual to another.

'Five hours sleepeth a traveller, seven a scholar, eight a merchant, and eleven every knave.'

So goes an old proverb, and there is much truth in proverbs. I must fall somewhere between merchant and knave. There are times when I like to rise early and times when I enjoy sleeping late. If I fall asleep before midnight, I will rise early.

One hour's sleep before midnight is worth two after. When the moon is up, the night has its magic; but at two or three in the morning there is very little to offer, because by ten even cats, bats and field-rats are asleep. In summer, bird-song starts at dawn, somewhere between four and five o'clock and that's a good time to be up and about, exercising mind or body.

The other morning I was up at five; wrote a couple of pages, opened my window and swallowed a portion of cloud;

closed it, conscience clear, and returned to bed where presently a cup of tea materialised, prepared by Beena or Dolly or some other member of the family. But for that morning cup of tea, would I have survived all these years? Without it, the mornings would be one long, endless wasteland. Without it, I would not get up. I would refuse breakfast, lunch and dinner, and waste away. Looking back upon my life from the vantage point of seventy years, I cannot remember a time when I was deprived of that morning cup of tea. Except for when I was in boarding school. Now you know why I ran away.

Getting up and making my own tea is no fun either. It has to be brought to me by some gentle soul—man, woman or child—who has got up before everyone else in order to ensure that I get up too.

The best tea I've ever drunk was made by an ex-convict who worked for my landlady in Dehradun, many years ago. He told me that while he was in jail he was assigned to the task of making the warden's tea. It was appreciated so much that they wouldn't let him go even after he'd served his sentence. How, then, did he gain his freedom? Well, my landlady was the wife of the jail superintendent. So you see how well the system worked!

For a while in London, I had a Jewish landlady who brought me my breakfast on a tray. I don't know if such civilised courtesies still exist. Back in the 1950s, English food was not very exciting; it had yet to be enriched by Indian curries and Chinese noodles. But breakfasts were always good—far superior to the skimpy fare served out by the French. Bacon and eggs, marmalade on toast, occasionally a kipper, a sausage, a slice of ham, grapefruit...what more could anyone ask for at the start of a busy day? And even now, when the days aren't quite so busy, I might skip lunch or dinner but I'll breakfast well.

So finally I'm out of bed and enjoying my breakfast. The children have gone to school and silence has descended on the house. A day in the life of Ruskin Bond is about to commence. I am at liberty to write a poem or a story or fill these pages with inconsequential thoughts. But first I must get dressed.

I am not fond of clothes, but I wouldn't care to start the day's work without at least wearing a clean shirt. When I was a struggling young writer, I did not possess more than two shirts at one time, but I would wash one every night in the hope that it would be dry by morning. Even today, I don't have a large wardrobe. It isn't possible, not with all these monkeys around. If you see a large red monkey wearing a blue and yellow check bush-shirt, please try and retrieve it for me; it's my favourite shirt. Putting clothes out on the roof to dry is fairly common practice in hill stations, but not to be recommended. Only the other day, when a strong wind came up from the east, I saw my pyjamas floating away downhill to end up entangled in the branches of an oak tree. Fortunately the milkman's son, who is good at climbing oak trees, rescued them for me. The milkman's son does not pass his exams, but as long as he can climb trees, he'll be a success in life. All of us need just one good accomplishment in order to get by. Obviously he can't spend the rest of his life climbing trees, but it's the agility and enterprise involved in the act that will make him a survivor.

Enough of bed and breakfast and getting ready for the long morning's journey into day. When does this ageing writer sit down to write? Or does he simply dictate to a secretary or into a machine of some kind? Well, I wish that was the case, because I'm a lazy sort of writer, better in bed than out of it. Unfortunately, I get tongue-tied when I try to tell a story, make a speech, or conduct something as simple as a telephone or cell phone conversation.

Recently Dolly made me buy a mobile phone; it would make me more efficient and up-to-date, she said. I tried making a call, and when nothing happened, she said, 'Dada, you're holding it upside down!' I got it the right way up and tried again, and when nothing happened, she said, 'Not here. You have to go to the window'

I dutifully walked over and tried again. No luck.
'Open the window,' ordered Dolly. I opened the window just a crackle on the cell phone. 'Now look out of the window!' I looked out, and there were all these schoolgirls gazing up at me, wondering why I was staring down at them. 'Good morning girls,' I called out, and gave them a friendly wave. 'No girls here,' said a gruff voice on the cell phone. 'This is your local thana.'

I gave the mobile to Dolly. She has no difficulty in getting through to her friends, or hearing from them. I'm no good at these things, except to pay the bill.

I'm strictly a man of the written word. Give me pen and paper and I manage to get something down, even if it's only for my own amusement. An elderly reader once remarked, 'How do you manage to write so much about nothing?' to which I could only reply: 'Well, it's better than writing nothing about everything!'

That small red ant walking across my desk may mean nothing to the world at large, but to me it represents the world at large. It represents industry, single-mindedness, intricacy of design, the perfection of nature, the miracle of creation. So much so, that it inspires me to poetic composition:

> You stride through the wasteland of my desk,
> Pressing on over books and papers,
> Down the wall and across the floor—
> Small red ant, now crossing a sea of raindrops
> At my open door.
> Your destiny, your task to carry home
> That heavy sunflower seed,
> Waving it like a banner
> Of victory!

Nothing is insignificant; nothing is without consequence in the intricate web of life.

# Travels with my Bank Manager

## 1

You couldn't ask for a livelier or more interesting companion than Ohri, my former bank manager. I say 'former', not because he is no longer with us, but because he has gone on to bigger and better things in Mumbai and Dubai where, I am given to understand, the streets are paved with gold. When I knew him he was a wildlife enthusiast with his heart in Corbett country and the Himalayan foothills.

Ohri liked travelling by road, preferably at dawn, the drive punctuated by halts to gaze at peacocks, nilghav, jackals and porcupines.

I'd accompany him occasionally, and one crisp winter morning we got into his battered old Fiat for a leisurely drive from Delhi to Dehradun. But Ohri had no intention of keeping to the main highway or doing anything in a leisurely manner.

'From Roorkee we'll take the Haridwar road, then take

a diversion and get onto the forest road through the Rajaji Sanctuary. We'll come out near the Mohand Pass. It is only about fifteen miles. Beautiful forest, lots of wildlife, tigers, herds of elephants, perfectly safe!'

'If you say so,' I said, not having much choice once he was behind the wheel.

By the time we had made it to the Rajaji forest road, dusk had fallen and the peahens were stridently calling up their mates.

There was three raos (dry river beds) to cross on the way to the pass, and at the first of these the front door threatened to come off its hinges.

'Hang on to it!' urged Ohri. 'Keep it from falling off!'

I had an old football scarf with me—a gift from travel writer Bill Aitken, a fellow fan of bottom of the Scottish League club, Alloa Athletic—and I tied this to the door handle, making it easier for me to keep the door from falling open.

Ohri stopped the car and pointed enthusiastically at several hefty dung-cakes in the middle of the road.

'Look, elephant dung!' he cried. 'Maybe we'll be lucky and see some wild elephants.'

'I'm quite content just viewing their leavings,' I said.

'Very good for making paper,' observed Ohri.

'Well, perhaps you could persuade the Reserve Bank to use the stuff for making notes, the large denominations.'

Undeterred by my sarcasm, Ohri started up and drove merrily into the second boulder-strewn rao. A bump, a bang, and we had a flat tyre.

'We'll soon fix it,' said Ohri. 'Will you get the spare tyre out of the dickey?'

Fortunately my struggle with the door prevented me from getting out, because just then a number of wild boars appeared at the side of the road. They had been in search of a little water in the rao and had now stopped in order to take a growing interest in the car and its occupants.

'Better wait until they've gone,' said Ohri. 'Wild boars can be dangerous. Even a tiger will run from a charging boar. Don't let the door fall off!'

I hung onto the door for dear life. I wasn't about to run like a tiger.

We waited. The boars waited.

'Would you like a drink?' asked Ohri after some time. 'There's a bottle here somewhere.'

He produced a full bottle of strong army rum and we took swigs in turn. The boars came a little nearer.

'If we're going to be here all night let's play Under a Scotsman's Kilt,' I suggested. 'I learnt it at school.'

'I didn't know you were gay.'

'I'm not. I'm serious. You give me the first line of a song or poem, and I'll come in with the line "Under a Scotman's Kilt." It's great fun. Don't think too hard. The first song that comes to mind...'

'Old Macdonald had a farm.'

'Under a Scotsman's kilt.'

'I wandered lonely as a cloud.'

'Under a Scotsman's kilt.'

'Tiger, tiger burning bright.'

'Under a Scotsman's kilt.'

We continued in this scatological vein for some time until,

fortunately for our sanity, the silence of the night was broken by the roar of an approaching motor-cycle. To our amazement, two middle-aged Sikh gentlemen materialised in front of our headlights. The wild boars scattered and vanished into the night.

Our rescuers were in the habit of using the forest road as a short-cut to their farm in the Terai.

Elephants and wild boars did not faze them. They helped us change the tyre, and then they helped us finish the bottle of rum. They even offered to get us another bottle, courtesy a helpful forest guard; but we thanked them profusely and said we had to be on our way. Ohri's wife was waiting for him in Dehradun, rolling pin at the ready. She would flatten him out along with the atta.

Ohri negotiated the remainder of the second rao and then, at the rao before Mohand, the door finally fell off, taking my Scottish football scarf with it.

Ever loyal to Alloa Athletic, I retrieved the scarf, but Ohri left the door behind in the river-bed.

'We'll come back for it another day,' he vowed. I was sure he had another treat in store for me.

**2**

The next time we met, a few weeks later, Ohri had a new car one of the latest Marutis.

'Come on, I'll take you for a spin down Tehri Road,' he said. 'We'll be back in time for lunch.'

'Are you sure?' I asked. 'I don't want to miss my afternoon siesta.'

'Nothing better than a nap under a chestnut tree,' said Ohri.

'The last time I slept under a chestnut tree, the langurs kept dropping chestnuts on my head. And this is October and the chestnuts are ready.'

'We'll go no further than Suakholi,' promised Ohri.

And so we set off in his new car, and on the way Ohri told me how he was having an ulcer problem and that Dr Bhist had told him to keep eating biscuits between meals. Apparently the biscuits soaked up the excess acid. On the seat between us I found three packets of biscuits—glucose, cream crackers and a third variety which I did not recognise.

'And what are these?' I asked.

'Dog biscuits,' he said.

'You're eating dog biscuits for your ulcer?'

'No, of course not. We have a dog now, a Labrador. My wife told me to bring home some dog biscuits.'

Ohri kept munching biscuits on the way to Suakholi, where we stopped for tea and more biscuits. 'Do we go home now?' I asked.

'Just a little further,' he urged. 'Don't you want to see the phosphate mines?'

I said I had no particular interest in phosphate mines, but he said we were sure to see some pheasants along the way, and so I let him talk me into an extension of the drive. A little way after Suakholi, we took a turning to the right, and continued along a rough dirt road which was obviously resented by the springs of Ohri's new car. We passed the phosphate mines, which appeared to have been shut down, and continued through a path of mixed forest in the general direction of the next mountain.

'This is not the way home,' I remarked.

'There's a forest rest house around the next bend,' said Ohri. 'Maybe the chowkidar can prepare some lunch for us.'

There was indeed a rest house around the bend, but it looked as though it hadn't been occupied for years. Most of the roof was missing. A wildcat spat at us from a broken wall. There was no sign of a chowkidar or any other human being.

'We'd better go back,' said Ohri. We shared the cream crackers and washed them down with mineral water. Ohri hadn't brought any rum along this time, which was just as well. He hadn't brought enough petrol, either. We hadn't gone very far when the over-taxed car spluttered to a stop.

'We should have turned back from Suakholi,' he said accusingly, as though it was all my fault.

'Well, you might get some in Suakholi,' I said. 'Ask a passing truck-driver. I'll stay here with the car.'

So Ohri trudged up to Suakholi, while I settled down in the shade of a whispering pine and enjoyed my afternoon siesta. When I woke up, it was evening and I was feeling hungry. I went to the car and through the window-glass saw that there were still some biscuits on the front seat. But Ohri had locked all the doors! I returned to the rest house and explored the ruins. There was nothing there that I could eat, except for some wild sorrel growing in the cracks of the building.

Ohri came back just as it was getting dark. He'd brought the petrol but had neglected to bring any food.

On our way back we ate the dog biscuits.

Try them sometime. They are really quite nourishing. And they don't taste too bad if you're really hungry.

When Ohri's wife scolded him for not bringing the dog

biscuits, all he could say was, 'Ruskin ate them.'

## 3

Banks are not normally exciting places, except when there's a bank robbery. But with Ohri around there was never a dull moment.

Our small branch is now computerised, but a few years ago it did not even have a typewriter. They used to borrow mine. Not everyday, but once a year, for a week or two, when their auditors came around.

I had three typewriters—a heavy Godrej, an old Olympic (which I still use occasionally) and an ancient German machine gifted to me by Goel, who is Swiss. The bank's chaprassi would walk down to my place, collect the Godrej, and struggle back up the hill with it. I did not share my Olympic with the bank. But on one occasion, while I was out, the chaprassi took the German machine by mistake and this led to some confusion.

On German typewriters the letter 'Z' occurs where there is normally a 'Y' on an English machine, and if you are not used to it, and are typing fast, you are apt to produce a certain amount of gibberish. If you want to say 'You might pick up yellow fever in Zanzibar', it could come out 'Zou might pick up yellow fever in Yanyibar'! The auditors and my friends at the bank got into many a tangle: zeros became yeros and even euros, Japanese yens became zens. Chinese yuans became zuans. The foreign exchange section was in a fine mess.

It was after this that the bank was hurriedly computerised.

Ohri had left by then. As a last treat he took me along on a nocturnal excursion to see a black panther which, he said, was on the prowl in the vicinity of Barlowganj.

'Black panthers are very rare now,' he told me. 'No one has seen one here in over fifty years!'

'Not since General Barlow shot the last one,' I added rather mischievously.

'We'll go down to Barlowganj tonight,' he said, as enthusiastic as ever. 'We'll sit up for it until dawn.'

'Don't forget the dog biscuits,' I said, 'I get hungry around midnight.'

Biscuits were not required. Mrs Ohri gave us a substantial dinner, guaranteed to put me to sleep while Ohri sat up looking for his black panther.

'It's just a big black dog,' she told me. 'The chowkidar at St George's school has a Bhotia mastiff. At night it gets mistaken for a panther.'

This wasn't going to deter Ohri from driving us down to the valley and back again, with numerous stops for panther-watching and swigs of rum. The stars looked down from a clear night sky. Ohri waxed poetic, 'The night has a thousand eyes—'

'Under a Scotsman's kilt,' I put in.

'Shh...we mustn't talk too much. We'll frighten it away.' 'If you see a panther, don't anther,' I quoted Ogden Nash. Ohri complained that I wasn't taking the expedition seriously, so I closed my eyes and fell asleep. Presently I was awake again. He was shaking me, whispering urgently, 'Look, there's something in those bushes, you can see them moving!'

They were indeed moving, and soon parted to reveal an elderly villager who had got up early in order to relieve himself in the great outdoors. He was not pleased at having his privacy disturbed.

'Have you seen a panther?' asked Ohri. 'Kala baghera?'

'Baghera yourself,' snapped the villager, who seemed equally at home in Hindi and English. 'Can't have a decent—in peace. Tourists all over the place,' and he stomped off into the darkness.

We were home before dawn. Mrs Ohri gave us a splendid breakfast.

'Did you see anything?' she asked.

'Too many people about,' I said. 'No room left for leopards, black or spotted.'

'We heard it,' insisted Ohri. 'I heard it growling in the bushes.'

'How do you know it was a black panther?' asked Mrs Ohri. 'It may have been spotted.'

'Not only that,' I added, 'it was carrying an empty mineral water bottle in lieu of a lota!'

# A Long Story

I live right on top of a hill and Gautam's school is right at the bottom; so I thought it would be a good idea if I walked the two miles to school with him every morning. I would be company for the boy, and the walk, I felt, would do wonders for my sagging waistline.

'Tell me a story,' he said the first time we set off together. And so I told him one. And the next day I told him another. A story a day, told on the long walk through the deodars became routine until I discovered that in this way I was writing myself out—that, story invented and told, I would come home to the realisation that the day's creative work was done and that I couldn't face my desk or typewriter.

So I decided it had to be a serial story. And I found that the best way to keep it going was to invent a man-eating leopard who carried off a different victim every day. An expanding population, I felt, could sustain his depredations over the months and even the years.

Small boys love blood-thirsty man-eaters, and Gautam was no exception. Every day, in the story, one of the townsfolk disappeared, a victim to the leopard's craving for human flesh. He started with the town gossip and worked his way through the clerk who'd lost my file, the barber who'd cut my hair too short, and the shopkeeper who'd sold me the previous year's fireworks, and well, there's no end to the people who can be visualised as suitable victims.

I must confess that I was getting as much pleasure out of the tale as Gautam. I think Freud might have had a theory or two about my attitude.

'When is it going to be shot?' asked Gautam one morning.

'Not yet,' I said, 'not yet.'

But towards the end of the year I was beginning to have qualms of conscience. Who was I, a mere mortal, to decide on who should be eaten and who should survive? Although the population had been reduced, the accommodation problem remained the same.

Well things came to a head when a real leopard appeared on the hillside and made off with my neighbour's pet pekinese.

Had I, with my fevered imaginings, brought into being an actual leopard? Only a dog-eater, true: but one never knew when it might start on people. And I was still well-fleshed, in spite of the long walks.

So the story had to end.

'The man-eater is dead,' I announced last week.

'Who shot it?'

'It wasn't shot. It just died.'

'Of old age?'

'No. Of ulcerative colitis.'

'What's that?' asked Gautam.

'Acute indigestion,' I said. 'It ate too many people.'

# Binya Passes By

The author looks back on a love of long ago. 'It isn't time that's passing by; it is you and I...'

While I was walking home one day, along the path through the pines, I heard a girl singing.

It was summer in the hills, and the trees were in new leaf. The walnuts and cherries were just beginning to form between the leaves.

The wind was still and the trees were hushed, and the song came to me clearly; but it was not the words—which I could not follow—or the rise and fall of the melody which held me in thrall, but the voice itself, which was a young and tender voice.

I left the path and scrambled down the slope, slipping on fallen pine needles. But when I came to the bottom of the slope, the singing had stopped and no one was there. 'I'm sure I heard someone singing,' I said to myself; but I may have been wrong. In the hills it is always possible to be wrong.

So I walked on home, and presently I heard another song, but this time it was the whistling thrush rendering a broken melody, singing of dark, sweet secrets in the depths of the forest.

I had little to sing about myself, as the electricity bill hadn't been paid, and there was nothing in the bank, and my second novel had just been turned down by another publisher. Still, it was summer, and men and animals were drowsy, and so too were my creditors. The distant mountains loomed purple in the shimmering dust-haze.

I walked through the pines again, but I did not hear the singing. And then for a week I did not leave the cottage, as the novel had to be rewritten, and I worked hard at it, pausing only to eat and sleep and take note of the leaves turning a darker green.

The window opened on to the forest. Trees reached up to the window. Oak, maple, walnut. Higher up the hill, the pines started, and further on, armies of deodars marched over the mountains. And the mountains rose higher, and the trees grew stunted until they finally disappeared and only the black spirit-haunted rocks rose up to meet the everlasting snows. Those peaks cradled the sky. I could not see them from my windows. But on clear mornings they could be seen from the pass on the Tehri road.

There was a stream at the bottom of the hill. One morning, quite early, I went down to the stream, and using the boulders as stepping-stones, moved downstream for about half a mile. Then I lay down to rest on a flat rock, in the shade of a wild cherry tree, and watched the sun shifting through the branches as it rose over the hill called Pari Tibba (Fairy Hill) and slid down the steep slope into the valley. The air was very still and already the birds were silent. The only sound came from the water running over the stony bed of the stream. I had lain there ten, perhaps fifteen, minutes when I began to feel that someone was watching me.

Someone in the trees, in the shadows, still and watchful. Nothing moved; not a stone shifted, not a twig broke; but someone was watching me. I felt terribly exposed; not to danger, but to the scrutiny of unknown eyes. So I left the rock and, finding a path through the trees, began climbing the hill again.

It was warm work. The sun was up, and there was no breeze. I was perspiring profusely by the time I got to the top of the hill. There was no sign of my unseen watcher. Two lean cows grazed on the short grass; the tinkling of their bells was the only sound in the sultry summer air.

That song again! The same song, the same singer. I heard her from my window. And putting aside the book I was reading, I leant out of the window and started down through the trees. But the foliage was too heavy, and the singer too far away for me to be able to make her out. 'Should I go and look for her?' I wondered. Or is it better this way—heard but not seen? For having fallen in love with a song, must it follow that I will fall in love with the singer? No. But surely it is the voice, and not the song that has touched me... Presently the singing ended, and I turned away from the window.

◆

A girl was gathering bilberries on the hillside. She was fresh-faced, honey-coloured; her lips were stained with purple juice.

She smiled at me. 'Are they good to eat?' I asked.

She opened her fist and thrust out her hand, which was full of berries, bruised and crushed. I took one and put it in my mouth. It had a sharp, sour taste. 'It is good,' I said. Finding that I could speak haltingly in her language, she came nearer, said, 'Take more then,' and filled my hand with bilberries. Her fingers touched mine. The sensation was almost unique; for it was nine or ten years since my hand had touched a girl's.

'Where do you live?' I asked. She pointed across the valley to where a small village straddled the slopes of a terraced hill.

'It's quite far,' I said. 'Do you always come so far from home?'

'I go further than this,' she said. 'The cows must find fresh grass. And there is wood to gather and grass to cut.' She showed me the sickle held by the cloth tied firmly about her waist. 'Sometimes I go to the top of Pari Tibba, sometimes to the valley beyond. Have you been there?'

'No. But I will go some day.'

'It is always windy on Pari Tibba.'

'Is it true that there are fairies there?'

She laughed. 'That is what people say. But those are people who have never been there. I do not see fairies on Pari Tibba. It is said that there are ghosts in the ruins on the hill. But I do not see any ghosts.'

'I have heard of the ghosts,' I said. 'Two lovers who ran away and took shelter in a ruined cottage. At night there was a storm, and they were killed by lightning. Is it true, this story?'

'It happened many years ago, before I was born. I have heard the story. But there are no ghosts on Pari Tibba.'

'How old are you?' I asked.

'Fifteen, sixteen, I do not know for sure.'

'Doesn't your mother know?'

'She is dead. And my grandmother has forgotten. And my brother, he is younger than me and he's forgotten his own age. Is it important to remember?'

'No, it is not important. Not here, anyway. Not in the hills. To a mountain, a hundred years are but as a day.'

'Are you very old?' she asked.

'I hope not. Do I look very old?'

'Only a hundred,' she said, and laughed, and the silver bangles on her wrists tinkled as she put her hand up to her laughing face.

'Why do you laugh?' I asked.

'Because you looked as though you believed me. How old are you?'

'Thirty-five, thirty-six, I do not remember.'

'Ah, it is better to forget!'

'That's true,' I said, 'but sometimes one has to fill in forms and things like that, and then one has to state one's age.'

'I have never filled a form. I have never seen one.'

'And I hope you never will. It is a piece of paper covered with useless information. It is all a part of human progress.'

'Progress?'

'Yes. Are you unhappy?'

'No.'

'Do you go hungry?'

'No.'

'Then you don't need progress. Wild bilberries are better.'

She went away without saying goodbye. The cows had strayed and she ran after them, calling them by name: 'Neelu,

Neelu!' (Blue) and 'Bhuri!' (Old One). Her bare feet moved swiftly over the rocks and dry grass.

◆

Early May. The cicadas were singing in the forests; or rather, orchestrating, since they make the sound with their legs. The whistling thrushes pursued each other over the tree-tops, in acrobatic love-flights. Sometimes the langurs visited the oak trees, to feed on the leaves. As I moved down the path to the stream, I heard the same singing; and coming suddenly upon the clearing near the water's edge, I saw the girl sitting on a rock, her feet in the rushing water—the same girl who had given me bilberries. Strangely enough, I had not guessed that she was the singer. Unseen voices conjure up fanciful images. I had imagined a woodland nymph, a graceful, delicate, beautiful, goddess-like creature; not a mischievous-eyed, round-faced, juice-stained, slightly ragged pixie. Her dhoti—a rough, homespun sari—faded and torn; an impractical garment, I thought, for running about on the hillside, but the village folk put their girls into dhotis before they are twelve. She'd compromised by hitching it up, and by strengthening the waist with a length of cloth bound tightly about her, but she'd have been more at ease in the long, flounced skirt worn in the further hills.

But I was not disillusioned. I had clearly taken a fancy to her cherubic, open countenance; and the sweetness of her voice added to her charms.

I watched her from the banks of the stream, and presently she looked up, grinned, and stuck her tongue out at me.

'That's a nice way to greet me,' I said. 'Have I offended you?'

'You surprised me. Why did you not call out?'

'Because I was listening to your singing. I did not wish to speak until you had finished.'

'It was only a song.'

'But you sang it sweetly.'

She smiled. 'Have you brought anything to eat?'

'No. Are you hungry?'

'At this time I get hungry. When you come to meet me you must always bring something to eat.'

'But I didn't come to meet you. I didn't know you would be here.'

'You do not wish to meet me?'

'I didn't mean that. It is nice to meet you.'

'You will meet me if you keep coming into the forest. So always bring something to eat.'

'I will do so next time. Shall I pick you some berries?'

'You will have to go to the top of the hill again to find the kingora bushes.'

'I don't mind. If you are hungry, I will bring some.'

'All right,' she said, and looked down at her feet, which were still in the water.

Like some knight-errant of old, I toiled up the hill again until I found the bilberry bushes; and stuffing my pockets with berries, I returned to the stream. But when I got there I found she'd slipped away. The cowbells tinkled on the far hill.

◆

Glow-worms shone fitfully in the dark. The night was full of sounds—the tonk-tonk of a nightjar, the cry of a barking deer, the shuffling of porcupines, the soft flip-flop of moths beating against the windowpanes. On the hill across the valley, lights flickered in the small village—the dim lights of kerosene lamps swinging in the dark.

'What is your name?' I asked, when we met again on the path through the pine forest.

'Binya,' she said. 'What is yours?'

'I've no name.'

'All right, Mr No-name.'

'I mean, I haven't made a name for myself. We must make our own names, don't you think?'

'Binya is my name. I do not wish to have any other. Where are you going?'

'Nowhere.'

'No-name goes nowhere! Then you cannot come with me, because I am going home and my grandmother will set the village dogs on you if you follow me.' And laughing, she ran down the path to the stream; she knew I could not catch up with her.

◆

Her face streamed summer rain as she climbed the steep hill, calling the white cow home. She seemed very tiny on the windswept mountainside; a twist of hair lay flat against her forehead, and her torn blue dhoti clung to her firm round thighs. I went to her with an umbrella to give her shelter. She stood with me beneath the umbrella and let me put my arm around her. Then she turned her face up to mine, wonderingly, and I kissed her quickly, softly on the lips. Her lips tasted of raindrops and mint. And then she left me there, so gallant in the blistering rain. She ran home laughing. But it was worth the drenching.

Another day I heard her calling to me—'No-name, Mister No-name!'—but I couldn't see her, and it was some time before I found her, halfway up a cherry tree, her feet pressed firmly against the bark, her dhoti tucked up between her thighs—fair, rounded thighs, and legs that were strong and vigorous.

'The cherries are not ripe,' I said.

'They are never ripe. But I like them green and sour. Will you come into the tree?'

'If I can still climb a tree,' I said.

'My grandmother is over sixty, and *she* can climb trees.'

'Well, I wouldn't mind being more adventurous at sixty. There's not so much to lose then.' I climbed into the tree without much difficulty, but I did not think the higher branches would take my weight; so I remained standing in the fork of the tree, my face on a level with Binya's breasts. I put my hand against her waist, and kissed her on the soft inside of her arm. She did not say anything. But she took me by the hand and helped me to climb a little higher, and I put my arm around her, as much to support myself as to be close to her.

◆

The full moon rides high, shining through the tall oak trees near the window. The night is full of sounds, crickets, the tonk-tonk of a nightjar, and floating across the valley from your village, the sound of drums beating, and people singing. It is a festival day, and there will be feasting in your home. Are you singing too, tonight? And are you thinking of me, as you sing, as you laugh, as you dance with your friends? I am sitting here alone, and so I have no one to think of but you.

Binya...I take your name again and again—as though by taking it, I can make you hear me, come to me, walking over the moonlit mountain...

There are spirits abroad tonight. They move silently in the trees; they hover about the window at which I sit; they take up with the wind and rush about the house. Spirits of the trees, spirits of the old house. An old lady died here last year. She'd lived in the house for over thirty years; something of her personality surely dwells here still. When I look into the tall, old mirror which was hers, I sometimes catch a glimpse of her pale face and long, golden hair. She likes me, I think, and the house is kind to me. Would she be jealous of you, Binya?

The music and singing grows louder. I can imagine your face glowing in the firelight. Your eyes shine with laughter. You have all those people near you and I have only the stars, and the nightjar, and the ghost in the mirror.

◆

I woke early, while the dew was still fresh on the grass, and walked down the hill to the stream, and then up to a little knoll where a pine tree grew in solitary splendour, the wind going *hoo-hoo* in its slender branches. This was my favourite place, my place of power, where I came to renew myself from time to time. I lay on the grass, dreaming. The sky in its blueness swung round above me. An eagle soared in the distance. I heard her voice down among the trees; or I thought I heard it. But when I went to look, I could not find her.

I'd always prided myself on my rationality; had taught

myself to be wary of emotional states, like 'falling in love', which turned out to be ephemeral and illusory. And although I told myself again and again that the attraction was purely physical, on my part as well as hers, I had to admit to myself that my feelings towards Binya differed from the feelings I'd had for others; and that while sex had often been for me a celebration, it had, like any other feast, resulted in satiety, a need for change, a desire to forget...

Binya represented something else—something wild, dream-like, fairy-like. She moved close to the spirit-haunted rocks, the old trees, the young grass; she had absorbed something from them—a primeval innocence, an unconcern with the passing of time and events, an affinity with the forest and the mountains; this made her special and magical.

And so, when three, four, five days went by, and I did not find her on the hillside, I went through all the pangs of frustrated love: had she forgotten me and gone elsewhere? Had we been seen together, and was she being kept at home? Was she ill? Or, had she been spirited away?

I could hardly go and ask for her. I would probably be driven from the village. It straddled the opposite hill, a cluster of slate-roof houses, a pattern of little terraced fields. I could see figures in the fields, but they were too far away, too tiny for me to be able to recognise anyone. She had gone to her mother's village a hundred miles away, or so a small boy told me.

And so I brooded; walked disconsolately through the oak forest hardly listening to the birds—the sweet-throated whistling thrush; the shrill barbet; the mellow-voiced doves. Happiness had always made me more responsive to nature. Feeling miserable, my thoughts turned inward. I brooded upon the trickery of time and circumstance; I felt the years were passing by, *had* passed by, like waves on a receding tide, leaving me washed up like a bit of flotsam on a lonely beach. But at the same time, the whistling thrush seemed to mock at me, calling tantalisingly from the shadows of the ravine; 'It isn't time that's passing by, it is you and I, it is you and I...'

Then I forced myself to snap out of my melancholy. I kept away from the hillside and the forest. I did not look towards the village. I buried myself in my work, tried to think objectively, and wrote an article on 'The inscriptions on the iron pillar at Kalsi'; very learned, very dry, very sensible.

But at night I was assailed by the thoughts of Binya. I could not sleep. I switched on the light, and there she was, smiling at me from the looking glass, replacing the image of the old lady who had watched over me for so long.

# The Kipling Road

Remember the old road,
The steep stony path
That took us up from Rajpur,
Toiling and sweating
And grumbling at the climb,
But enjoying it all the same.
At first the hills were hot and bare,
But then there were trees near Jharipani
And we stopped at the Halfway House
And swallowed lungfuls of diamond-cut air.
Then onwards, upwards, to the town,
Our appetites to repair!

Well, no one uses the old road anymore.
Walking is out of fashion now.
And if you have a car to take you
Swiftly up the motor-road

Why bother to toil up a disused path?

You'd have to be an old romantic like me
To want to take that route again.
But I did it last year,
Pausing and plodding and gasping for air-
Both road and I being a little worse for wear!
But I made it to the top and stopped to rest
And looked down to the valley and the silver stream
Winding its way towards the plains.
And the land stretched out before me, and the years fell away,
And I was a boy again,
And the friends of my youth were there beside me,
And nothing had changed.

'Remember the Old Road'

As boys we would often trudge up from Rajpur to Mussoorie by the old bridle-path, the road that used to serve the hillstation in the days before the motor road was built. Before 1900, the traveller to Mussoorie took a tonga from Saharanpur to Dehradun, spent the night at a Rajpur hotel, and the following day came up the steep seven-mile path on horseback, or on foot, or in a dandy (a crude palanquin) held aloft by two, sometimes four, sweating coolies.

The railway came to Dehradun in 1904, and a few years later the first motor car made it to Mussoorie, the motor road following the winding contours and hairpin bends of the old bullock-cart road. Rajpur went out of business; no one stopped there any more, the hotels became redundant, and the bridlepath was seldom used except by those of us who thought it would be fun to come up on foot.

For the first two or three miles you walked in the hot sun, along a treeless path. It was only at Jharipani (at approximately 4,000 ft.) that the oak forests began, providing shade and shelter. Situated on a spur of its own, was the Railways school, Oakgrove, still there today, providing a boarding-school education to the children of Railway personnel. My mother and her sisters came from a Railway family, and all of them studied at Oakgrove in the 1920s. So did a male cousin, who succumbed to cerebral malaria during the school term. In spite of the salubrious climate, mortality was high amongst school children. There were no cures then for typhoid, cholera, malaria, dysentery and other infectious diseases.

Above Oakgrove was Fairlawn, the palace of the Nepali royal family. There was a sentry box outside the main gate, but there was never any sentry in it, and on more than one occasion I took shelter there from the rain. Today it's a series of cottages, one of which belongs to Outlook's editor, Vinod Mehra, who seeks shelter there from the heat and dust of Delhi.

From Jharapani we climbed to Barlowganj, where another venerable institution St George's College, crowns the hilltop. Then on to Bala Hissar, once the home-in-exile of an Afghan king, and now the grounds of Wynberg-Allen, another school, In later years I was to live near this school, and it was its then Principal, Rev W Biggs, who told me that the bridle-path was once known as the Kipling Road.

Why was that, I asked. Had Kipling ever come up that way? Rev Biggs wasn't sure, but he referred me to Kim, and the chapter in which Kim and the Lama leave the plains for the hills. It begins thus:

> They had crossed the Siwaliks and the half-tropical
> Doon, left Mussoorie behind them, and headed north
> along the narrow hill-roads. Day after day they struck
> deeper into the huddled mountains, and day after day
> Kim watched the lama return to a man's strength.
> Among the terraces of the Doon he had leaned on
> the boy's shoulder, ready to profit by wayside halts.
> Under the great ramp to Mussoorie he drew himself
> together as an old hunter faces a well remembered bank,
> and where he should have sunk exhausted swung his
> long draperies about him, drew a deep double-lungful
> of the diamond air, and walked as only a hillman can.

This description is accurate enough, but it is not evidence that
Kipling actually came this way, and his geography becomes quite
confusing in the subsequent pages—as peter hopkirk discovered
when he visited Mussoorie a few years ago, retracing Kim's
journeys for his book *Quest for Kim*. Hopkirk spent some time
with me in this little room where I am now writing, but we were
unable to establish the exact route that Kim and the Lama took
after traversing Mussoorie. Presumably they had come up the
bridle-path. But then? After that, Kipling becomes rather vague.

Mussoorie does not really figure in Rudyard Kipling's prose
or poetry. The Simla Hills were his beat. As a journalist he was a
regular visitor to Simla, then the summer seat of the British Raj.

But last year my Swiss friend, Anilees Goel, brought me
proof that Kipling had indeed visited Mussoorie. Among his
unpublished papers and other effects in the Library of Congress,
there exists an album of photographs, which includes two of the

Charleville Hotel, Mussoorie, where he had spent the summer of 1888. On a photograph of the office he had inscribed these words:

> And there were men with a thousand wants
> And women with babes galore
> But the dear little angels in Heaven know
> That Wutzler *never* swore.

Wutzler was the patient, long-suffering manager of this famous hotel, now the premises of the Lal Bahadur Shastri National Academy of Administration.

A second photograph is inscribed with the caption 'Quarters at the Charleville, April July 88', and carries this verse:

> A burning sun in cloudless skies
>    and April dies,
> A dusty Mall—three sunsets splendid
>    and May is ended,
> Grey mud beneath-grey cloud o'erhead
>    and June is dead.
> A little bill in late July
>    And then we fly.

Pleasant enough, but hardly great verse, and I'm not surprised that Kipling did not publish these lines.

However, we now know that he came to Mussoorie and spent some time here, and that he would have come up by the old bridle-path (there was no other way except by bullock-cart on the long and tortuous cast road), and Rev Biggs and others were right in calling it the Kipling Road, although officially that was never its name.

As you climb up from Barlowganj, you pass a number of pretty cottages—May Cottage, Wakefield, Ralston Manor, Wayside Hall—and these old houses all have stories to tell, for they have stood mute witness to the comings and goings of all manner of people.

Take Ralston Manor. It was witness to an impromptu cremation, probably Mussoorie's first European cremation, in the late 1890s. There is a small chapel in the grounds of Ralston, and the story goes that a Mr and Mrs Smallman had been living in the house, and Mr Smallman had expressed a wish to be cremated at his death. When he died, his widow decided to observe his wishes and had her servants build a funeral pyre in the garden. The cremation was well underway when someone rode by and looked in to see what was happening. The unauthorised cremation was reported to the authorities and Mrs Smallman had to answer some awkward questions. However, she was let off with a warning (a warning not to cremate any future husbands?) and later she built the little chapel on the site of the funeral pyre—in gratitude or as penance, or as a memorial, we are not told. But the chapel is still there, and this little tale is recorded in Chowkidar (Autumn 1995), the journal of the British Association for Cemeteries in South Asia (BACSA).

As we move further up the road, keeping to the right, we come to Wayside Hall and Wayside Cottage, which have the advantage of an open sunny hillside and views to the north and east. I lived in the cottage for a couple of years, back in 1966-67, as a tenant of the Powell sisters who lived in the Hall.

There were three sisters, all in their seventies; they had

survived their husbands. Annie, the eldest, had a son who lived abroad; Martha, the second, did not have children; Dr Simmonds, the third sister, had various adopted children who came to see her from time to time. They were God-fearing, religious folk, but not bigots; never chided me for not going to church. Annie's teas were marvellous; snacks and savouries in abundance.

They kept a beautiful garden.

'Why go to church?' I said. 'Your garden is a church.'

In spring and summer it was awash with poppies, petunia, phlox, larkspur, calendula, snapdragons and other English flowers. During the monsoon, the gladioli took over, while magnificent dahlias reared up from the rich foliage. During the autumn came zinnias and marigolds and cosmos. And even during the winter months there would be geraniums and primulae blooming in the verandah.

Honeysuckle climbed the wall outside my window, filling my bedroom with its heady scent. And wisteria grew over the main gate. There was perfume in the air.

Annie herself smelt of freshly baked bread. Dr Simmonds smelt of Pears' baby soap. Martha smelt of apples. All good smells, emanating from good people.

Although they lived on their own, without any men on the premises, they never felt threatened or insecure. Mussoorie was a safe place to live in then, and still is to a great extent, much safer than towns in the plains, where the crime rate keeps pace with the population growth.

Annie's son, Gerald, then in his sixties, did come out to see them occasionally. He had been something of a shikari in his youth—or so he claimed—and told me he could call up a panther from the valley without any difficulty. To do this, he made a contraption out of an old packing-case, with a hole bored in the middle, then he passed a length of thick wire through the hole, and by moving the wire backwards and forward produced a sound not dissimilar to the sawing, coughing sound made by a panther during the mating season. (Incidentally, a panther and a leopard are the same animal.)

Gerry invited me to join him on a steep promontory overlooking a little stream. I did so with some trepidation. Hunting had never been my forte, and normally I preferred to go along with Ogden Nash's dictum, 'If you meet a panther, don't anther!'

However, Gerry's gun looked powerful enough, and I believed him when he told me he was a crack shot. I have always taken people at their word. One of my failings I suppose.

Anyway, we positioned ourselves on this ledge, and Gerry started producing panther noises with his box. His Master's Voice would have been proud of it. Nothing happened for about twenty minutes, and I was beginning to lose patience when we were answered by the cough and grunt of what could only have been a panther. But we couldn't see it! Gerry produced a pair of binoculars and trained them on some distant object below, which turned out to be a goat. The growling continued, and then it was just above us! The panther had made a detour and was now standing on a rock and staring down, no doubt wondering which of us was making such attractive mating calls.

Gerry swung round, raised his gun and fired. He missed by a couple of feet, and the panther bounded away, no doubt disgusted with the proceedings.

We returned to Wayside Hall, and revived ourselves with brandy and soda.

'We'll get it next time, old chap,' said Gerry. But although we tried, the panther did not put in another appearance. Gerry's panther call sounded genuine enough, but neither he nor I nor his wired box looked anything like a female panther.

# Trees by my Window

L iving at seven thousand feet, I am fortunate to have a big
window that opens out on the forest so that the trees are
almost within my reach. If I jumped, I could land quite neatly
in the arms of an oak or horse chestnut. I have never made
that leap, but the big langurs—silver-gray monkeys with long,
swishing tails—often spring from the trees onto my corrugated
tin roof, making enough noise to frighten all the birds away.

Standing on its own outside my window is a walnut tree,
and truly this is a tree for all seasons. In winter the branches
are bare, but beautifully smooth and rounded. In spring each
limb produces a bright green spear of new growth, and by
mid-summer the entire tree is in leaf. Toward the end of the
monsoon the walnuts, encased in their green jackets, have
reached maturity. When the jackets begin to split, you can see
the hard brown shells of the nuts, and inside each shell is the
delicious meat itself.

Every year this tree gives me a basket of walnuts. But last

year the nuts were disappearing one by one, and I was at a loss as to who had been taking them. Could it have been the milkman's small son? He was an inveterate tree climber, but he was usually to be found on the oak trees, gathering fodder for his herd. He admitted that his cows had enjoyed my dahlias, which they had eaten the previous week, but he stoutly denied having fed them walnuts.

It wasn't the woodpecker either. He was out there every day, knocking furiously against the bark of the tree, trying to pry an insect out of a narrow crack, but he was strictly nonvegetarian. As for the langurs, they ate my geraniums but did not care for the walnuts.

The nuts seemed to disappear early in the morning while I was still in bed, so one day I surprised everyone, including myself, by getting up before sunrise. I was just in time to catch the culprit climbing out of the walnut tree. She was an old woman who sometimes came to cut grass on the hillside. Her face was as wrinkled as the walnuts she so fancied, but her arms and legs were very sturdy.

'And how many walnuts did you gather today, Grandmother?' I asked.

'Just two,' she said with a giggle, offering them to me on her open palm. I accepted one, and thus encouraged, she climbed higher into the tree and helped herself to the remaining nuts. It was impossible for me to object. I was taken with admiration for her agility. She must have been twice my age, but I knew I could never get up that tree. To the victor, the spoils!

Unlike the prized walnuts, the horse chestnuts are inedible. Even the rhesus monkeys throw them away in disgust. But the tree itself is a friendly one, especially in summer when it is in full leaf. The lightest breeze makes the leaves break into conversation, and their rustle is a cheerful sound. The spring flowers of the horse chestnut look like candelabra, and when the blossoms fall, they carpet the hillside with their pale pink petals.

Another of my favorites is the deodar. It stands erect and dignified and does not bend with the wind. In spring the new leaves, or needles, are a tender green, while during the monsoon the tiny young cones spread like blossoms in the dark green folds of the branches. The deodar enjoys the company of its own kind: where one deodar grows, there will be others. A walk in a deodar forest is awe-inspiring—surrounded on all sides by these great sentinels of the mountains, you feel as though the trees themselves are on the march.

I walk among the trees outside my window often, acknowledging their presence with a touch of my hand against their trunks. The oak has been there the longest, and the wind has bent its upper branches and twisted a few so that it looks shaggy and undistinguished. But it is a good tree for the privacy of birds. Sometimes it seems completely uninhabited until there is a whirring sound, as of a helicopter approaching, and a party of long-tailed blue magpies flies across the forest glade.

Most of the pines near my home are on the next hillside. But there is a small Himalayan blue a little way below the cottage, and sometimes I sit beneath it to listen to the wind playing softly in its branches.

When I open the window at night, there is almost always something to listen to: the mellow whistle of a pygmy owlet, or the sharp cry of a barking deer. Sometimes, if I am lucky,

I will see the moon coming up over the next mountain, and two distant deodars in perfect silhouette.

Some night sounds outside my window remain strange and mysterious. Perhaps they are the sounds of the trees themselves, stretching their limbs in the dark, shifting a little, flexing their fingers, whispering to one another. These great trees of the mountains, I feel they know me well, as I watch them and listen to their secrets, happy to rest my head beneath their outstretched arms.

# Road to Badrinath

If you have travelled up the Mandakini valley, and then cross over into the valley of the Alaknanda, you are immediately struck by the contrast. The Mandakini is gentler, richer in vegetation, almost pastoral in places; the Alaknanda is awesome, precipitous, threatening, and seemingly inhospitable to those who must live and earn a livelihood in its confines.

Even as we left Chamoli and began the steady, winding climb to Badrinath, the nature of the terrain underwent a dramatic change. No longer did green fields slope gently down to the riverbed. Here they clung precariously to rocky slopes and ledges that grew steeper and narrower, while the river below, impatient to reach its confluence with the Bhagirathi at Deoprayag, thundered along a narrow gorge.

Badrinath is one of the four Dhams, or four most holy places in India (the other three are Rameshwaram, Dwarka and Jagannath Puri). For the pilgrim travelling to his holiest of holies, the journey is exciting, possibly even uplifting; but for those who live permanently on these crags and ridges, life is harsh, a struggle from one day to the next. No wonder so many young men from Garhwal make their way into the Army. Little grows on these rocky promontories; and what does is at the mercy of the weather. For most of the year the fields lie fallow. Rivers, unfortunately, run downhill and not uphill.

The harshness of this life, typical of much of Garhwal, was brought home to me at Pipalkoti, where we stopped for the night. Pilgrims stop here by the coachload, for the Garhwal Mandal Vikas Nigam's rest house is fairly capacious and small hotels and dharamsalas abound. Just off the busy road is a tiny hospital, and here, late in the evening, we came across a woman keeping vigil over the dead body of her husband. The body had been laid out on a bench in the courtyard. A few feet away the road was crowded with pilgrims in festival mood; no one glanced over the low wall to notice this tragic scene.

The woman came from a village near Helong. Earlier that day, finding her consumptive husband in a critical condition, she had decided to bring him to the nearest town for treatment. As he was frail and emaciated, she was able to carry him on her back for several miles until she reached the motor road. Then, at some expense, she engaged a passing taxi and brought him to Pipalkoti. But he was already dead when she reached the small hospital. There was no morgue; so she sat beside the body in the courtyard, waiting for dawn and the arrival of others from the village. A few men arrived next morning, and we saw them wending their way down to the cremation ground. We did not see the woman again. Her children were hungry and she had to hurry home to look after them.

Pipalkoti is hot (and pipal trees are conspicuous by their absence), but Joshimath, the winter resort of the Badrinath temple establishment, is about 6,000 ft above sea-level and has an equable climate. It is now a fairly large town, and although the surrounding hills are rather bare, it does have one great tree that has survived the ravages of time. This is an ancient mulberry, known as the Kalpa-Vriksha (Immortal Wishing Tree), beneath which the great Sankaracharya meditated a few centuries ago. It is reputedly over two thousand years old, and is certainly larger than my modest four-roomed flat in Mussoorie. Sixty pilgrims holding hands might just about encircle its trunk.

I have seen some big trees, but this is certainly the oldest and broadest of them. I am glad that Sankaracharya meditated beneath it and thus ensured its preservation. Otherwise it might well have gone the way of other great trees and forests that once flourished in this area.

A small boy reminds me that it is a Wishing Tree, so I make my wish. I wish that other trees might prosper like this.

'Have you made a wish?' I ask the boy.

'I wish that you will give me one rupee,' he says.

His wish comes true with immediate effect. Mine lies in an uncertain future. But he has given me a lesson in wishing.

Joshimath has to be a fairly large place because most of Badrinath arrives here in November, when the shrine is snowbound for six months. Army and PWD structures also dot the landscape. This is no carefree hill resort, but it has all the amenities for making a short stay quite pleasant and interesting. Perched on the steep mountainside above the junction of the Alaknanda and Dhauli rivers, it is now vastly different from what it was when Frank Smythe visited it fifty years ago and described it as 'an ugly little place...straggling unbeautifully over the hillside. Primitive little shops line the main street, which is roughly paved in places and in others has been deeply channelled by the monsoon rains. The pilgrims spend the night in single-storeyed rest houses, not unlike the hovels provided for the Kentish hop-pickers of former days, and are filthy and evil-smelling'.

Those were Joshimath's former days. It is a different place today, with small hotels, modern shops, a cinema; and its growth and comparative modernity dates from the early sixties when the old pilgrim footpath gave way to the motor road which takes the traveller all the way to Badrinath. No longer does the weary, footsore pilgrim sink gratefully down in the shade of the Kalpa-Vriksha. He alights from his bus or luxury coach and drinks a Cola or a Thums-up at one of the many small restaurants on the roadside.

Contrast this comfortable journey with the pilgrimage fifty years ago. Frank Smythe again: 'So they venture on their pilgrimage... Some borne magnificently by coolies, some toiling along in rags, some almost crawling, preyed on by disease and distorted by dreadful deformities...Europeans who have read and travelled cannot conceive what goes on in the minds of these simple folk, many of them from the agricultural parts of India. Wonderment and fear must be the prime ingredients. So the pilgrimage becomes an adventure. Unknown dangers threaten the broad well-made path, at any moment the Gods, who hold the rocks in leash, may unloose their wrath upon the hapless passerby. To the European it is a walk to Badrinath, to the Hindu pilgrim it is far, far more.'

Above Vishnuprayag, Smythe left the Alaknanda and entered the Bhyundar valley, a botanist's paradise, which he called the Valley of Flowers. He fell in love with the lush meadows of this high valley and made it known to the world. It continues to attract the botanist and trekker. Primulas of subtle shades, wild geraniums, saxifrages clinging to the rocks, yellow and red potentillas, snow-white anemones, delphiniums, violets, wild roses, all these and many more flourish there, capturing the mind and heart of the flower-lover.

'Impossible to take a step without crushing a flower.' This may not be true any more, for many footsteps have trodden the Bhyundar in recent years. There are other areas in Garhwal where the hills are rich in flora—the Har-ki-Doon, Harsil, Tungnath, and the Khiraun valley where the Balsam grows to a height of eight feet—but the Bhyundar has both a variety and a concentration of wild flowers, especially towards the end of the monsoon. It would be no exaggeration to call it one of the most beautiful valleys in the world.

The Bhyundar is a digression for lovers of mountain scenery; but the pilgrim keeps his eyes fixed on the ultimate goal— Badrinath, where the gods dwell and where salvation is to be found.

There are still a few who do it the hard way—mostly those who have taken sanyas and renounced the world. Here is one hardy soul doing penance. He stretches himself out on the ground, draws himself up to a standing position, then flattens himself out again. In this manner he will proceed from Badrinath to Rishikesh, oblivious of the sun and rain, the dust from passing buses, the sharp gravel of the footpath.

Others are not so hardy. One saffron-robed scholar speaking fair English asks us for a lift to Badrinath, and we find a space for him. He rewards us with a long and involved commentary on the Vedas, which lasts through the remainder of the journey. His special field of study, he informs us, is the part played by Aeronautics in Vedic literature.

'And what,' I ask him, 'is the connection between the two?'

He looks at me pityingly.

'It is what I am trying to find out,' he replies.

The road drops to Pandukeshwar and rises again, and all the time I am scanning the horizon for the forests of the Badrinath region I had read about many years ago in Eraser's *Himalaya Mountains*. Walnuts growing up to 9,000 ft, deodars and Bilka up to 9,500 ft, and Amesh and Kiusu fir to a similar height—but, apart from strands of long leaved and excelsia pine, I do not see much, certainly no deodars. What has happened to them, I wonder. An endless variety of trees delighted us all the way from Dugalbeta to Mandal, a well-protected area, but here on the high ridges above the Alaknanda, little seems to grow: or, if ever anything did, it has long since been bespoiled or swept away.

Finally we reach the windswept, barren valley which harbours Badrinath—a growing township, thriving, lively, but somewhat dwarfed by the snow-capped peaks that tower above it. As at Joshimath, there is no dearth of hostelries and dharamsalas. Even so, every hotel or rest house is overcrowded. It is the height of the pilgrim season, and pilgrims, tourists and mendicants of every description throng the river-front.

Just as Kedar is the most sacred of the Shiva temples in the

Himalayas, similarly Badrinath is the supreme place of worship
for the Vaishnav sects.

According to legend, when Sankaracharya in his Digvijaya
travels visited the Mana valley, he arrived at the Narada-Kund
and found fifty different images lying in its waters. These he
rescued, and when he had done so, a voice from Heaven said:
'These are the images for the Kaliyug, establish them here.'
Sankaracharya accordingly placed them beneath a mighty tree
which grew there and whose shade extended from Badrinath to
Nandprayag, a distance of over eighty miles. Close to it was the
hermitage of Nar-Nandprayag (or Arjuna and Krishna), and in
course of time temples were built in honour of these and other
manifestations of Vishnu. It was here that Vishnu appeared to
his followers in person, as four-armed, crested and adorned with
pearls and garlands. The faithful, it is said, can still see him on
the peak of Nilkantha, on the great Kumbha day. It is in fact
the Nilkantha peak that dominates this crater-like valley, where
a few hardy thistles and nettles manage to survive. Like cacti
in the desert, the pricklier forms of life seem best equipped to
live in a hostile environment.

Nilkantha means blue-necked, an allusion to Lord Shiva's
swallowing of a poison meant to destroy the world. The poison
remained in his throat, which was rendered blue thereafter. It is a
majestic and awe-inspiring peak, soaring to a height of 21,640 ft.
As its summit is only five miles from Badrinath, it is justly held
in reverence. From its ice-clad pinnacle, three great ridges sweep
down, of which the south terminates in the Alaknanda valley.

On the evening of our arrival we could not see the peak,
as it was hidden in cloud. Badrinath itself was shrouded in

mist. But we made our way to the temple, a gaily decorated building, about fifty feet high, with a gilded roof. The image of Vishnu, carved in black stone, stands in the centre of the sanctum, opposite the door, in a Dhyana posture. An endless stream of people pass through the temple to pay homage and emerge the better for their proximity to the divine.

From the temple, flights of steps lead down to the rushing river and to the hot springs which emerge just above it. Another road leads through a long but tidy bazaar where pilgrims may buy mementos of their visit—from sacred amulets to pictures of the gods in vibrant technicolour. Here at last I am free to indulge my passion for cheap rings, with none to laugh at my foible. There are all kinds, from rings designed like a coiled serpent (my favourite) to twisted bands of copper and iron and others containing the pictures of gods, gurus and godmen. They do not cost more than two or three rupees each, and so I am able to fill my pockets. I never wear these rings. I simply hoard them away. My friends are convinced that in a previous existence I was a jackdaw, seizing upon and hiding away any kind of bright and shiny object!

India is a land of crowds, and it is no different at Badrinath where people throng together, all in good spirits. Hindus enjoy their religion. Whether bathing in cold streams or hot springs, or tramping from one sacred mountain shrine to another, they are united in their wish to experience something of the magic and mystique of the gods and glories of another epoch.

Even those who have renounced the world appear to be cheerful—like the young woman from Gujarat who had taken sanyas, and who met me on the steps below the temple. She gave me a dazzling smile and passed me an exercise book. She had taken a vow of silence; but being, I think, of an extrovert nature, she seemed eager to remain in close communication with the rest of humanity, and did so by means of written questions and answers. Hence the exercise book. Together we filled three pages of it before she told me that she wished to proceed on pilgrimage to Amarnath but was short of funds. With help from my generous companion, we made her a donation, and with a flashing smile of thanks she left us and was lost in the crowd.

Although at Badrinath I missed the sound of birds and the presence of trees, there were other compensations. It was good to be part of the happy throng at its colourful little temple and to see the sacred river close to its source. And early next morning I was rewarded with the loveliest experience of all.

Opening the window of my room and glancing out, I saw the rising sun touch the snow-clad summit of Nilkantha. At first the snows were pink; then they turned to orange and gold. All sleep vanished as I gazed up in wonder at that magnificent pinnacle in the sky. And had Lord Vishnu appeared just then on the summit, I would not have been in the least surprised.

# In Search of Sweet Peas

If someone were to ask me to choose between writing an essay on the Taj Mahal or on the last rose of the summer, I'd take the rose—even if it was down to its last petal. Beautiful, cold, white marble leaves me—well, just a little cold… Roses are warm and fragrant, and almost every flower I know, wild or cultivated, has its own unique quality, whether it be subtle fragrance or arresting colour or liveliness of design. Unfortunately, winter has come to the Himalayas, and the hillsides are now brown and dry, the only colour being that of the red sorrel growing from the limestone rocks. Even my small garden looks rather forlorn, with the year's last dark-eyed nesturtium looking every bit like the Lone Ranger surveying the surrounding wilderness from his saddle. The marigolds have dried in the sun and tomorrow I will gather the seeds. The beanstalk that grew rampant during the monsoon is now down to a few yellow leaves and empty bean-pods.

'This won't do,' I told myself the other day. 'I must have

flowers.' Prem, who had been to the valley town of Dehra the previous week, had made me even more restless, because he had spoken of masses of sweet-peas in full bloom in the garden of one of the town's public schools. Down in the plains, winter is the best time for gardens, and I remembered my grandmother's house in Dehra, with its long rows of hollyhocks, neatly-stalked sweet-peas and beds ablaze with red salvia and antirrhinum. Neither grandmother nor the house are there anymore. But surely there are other beautiful gardens, I mused, and maybe I could visit the school where Prem had seen the sweet-peas. It was a long time since I had enjoyed their delicate fragrance.

So I took the bus down the hill, and throughout the two-hour journey, I dozed and dreamt of gardens—cottage gardens in the English countryside, tropical gardens in Florida, Mughal gardens in Kashmir, the Hanging Gardens of Babylon—what had they been like, I wondered.

And then we were in Dehra, and I got down from the bus and walked down the dusty, busy road to the school Prem had told me about.

It was encircled by a high wall, and, tip-toeing, I could see playing fields and extensive school buildings and, in the far distance, a dollop of colour which may have been a garden. Prem's eyesight was obviously better than mine.

Anyway, I made my way to a wrought iron gate that would have done justice to a medieval fortress, and found it chained and locked. On the other side stood a tough looking guard, with a rifle.

'May I enter?' I asked.

'Sorry, sir, today is holiday. No school today.'

'I don't want to attend classes, I want to see the sweet-peas.'

'Kitchen is on the other side of the ground.'

'Not green peas. Sweet-peas. I'm looking for the garden.'

'I am guard here.'

'Garden.'

'No garden, only guard.'

I tried telling him that I was an old boy of the school and that I was visiting the town after a long interval. This was true up to a point, because I had once been admitted to this very school, and after one day's attendance had insisted on going back to my old school. The guard was unimpressed. And perhaps it was poetic justice that the gates were barred to me now.

Disconsolate, I strolled down the main road, past a garage, a cinema, a row of cheap eating houses and tea shops. Behind the shops there seemed to be a park of sorts, but you couldn't see much of it from the road because of the buildings, the press of the people, and the passing trucks and buses. But I found the entrance, unbarred this time, and struggled through patches of overgrown shrubbery until, like Alice after finding the golden key to the little door in the wall, I looked upon a lovely little garden.

There were no sweet-peas, true, and the small fountain was dry. But around it, filling a large circular bed, were masses of bright yellow Californian poppies!

They stood out like sunshine after the rain, and my heart leapt as Wordsworth's must have done when he saw his daffodils. I found myself oblivious to the sounds of the bazaar and the road, just as the people outside seemed oblivious to this little garden. It was as though it had been waiting here all the time.

Waiting for me to come by and discover it.

I am very fortunate. Something like this is always happening to me. As grandmother often said, 'When one door closes, another door opens.' And while one gate had been closed upon the sweet-peas, another had opened on Californian poppies.

◆

Trees make you feel younger. And the older the tree, the younger you feel.

Whenever I pass beneath the old tamarind tree standing sentinel in the middle of Dehra's busiest street crossing, the years fall away and I am a boy again, sitting on the railing that circled the tree, while across the road, Granny ascended the steps of the Allahabad Bank, where she kept her savings.

The bank is still there, but the surroundings have changed, the traffic and the noise is far greater than it used to be, and I wouldn't dream of sauntering across the road as casually as I would have done in those days. The press of people is greater too, reflecting the tenfold increase in population that has taken place in this and other north Indian towns during the last forty years. But the old tamarind has managed to survive it all. As long as it stands, as long as its roots still cling to Debra's rich soil, I shall feel confident that my own roots are well embedded in this old valley town.

There was a time when almost every Indian village had its spreading banyan tree, in whose generous shade, schoolteachers conducted open-air classes, village elders met to discuss matters of moment, and itinerant merchants spread out their ware. Squirrels, birds of many kinds, flying-foxes, and giant beetles, are just some, of the many inhabitants of this gentle giant. Ancient banyan trees are still to be found in some parts of the country; but as villages grow into towns, and towns into cities, the banyan is gradually disappearing. It needs a lot of space for its aerial roots to travel and support it, and space is now at a premium.

If you can't find a banyan, a mango grove is a wonderful place for a quiet stroll or an afternoon siesta. In traditional paintings, it is often the haunt of young lovers. But if the mangoes are ripening, there is not much privacy in a mango grove. Parrots, crows, monkeys and small boys are all attempting to evade the watchman who uses an empty gasoline tin as a drum to frighten away these intruders.

The mango and the banyan don't grow above the foothills, and here in the mountains, the more familiar trees are the Himalayan oaks, horse-chestnuts, rhododendrons, pines and deodars. The deodar (from the Sanskrit dev-dar, meaning Tree of God) resembles the cedar of Lebanon, and can grow to a great height in a few hundred years. There are a number of giant deodars on the outskirts of Mussoorie, where I live, and they make the town seem quite young. Mussoorie is only 160 years old. The deodars are at least twice that age.

These are gregarious trees—they like being among their own kind—and a forest of deodars is an imposing sight. When a mountain is covered with them, they look like an army on the march: the only kind of army one would like to see marching over the mountains! Although the world has already lost over half its forest cover, these sturdy giants look as though they are going to be around a long time, given half a chance.

The world's oldest trees, a species of pine, grow in California and have been known to live up to five thousand years. Is that why Californians look so young?

The oldest tree I have seen is an ancient mulberry growing at Joshimath, a small temple town in the Himalayas. It is known as the Kalp-Vriksha or Immortal Tree. The Hindu sage, Sankaracharya, is said to have meditated beneath it in the sixteenth century. These ancient sages always found a suitable tree beneath which they could meditate. The Buddha favoured a banyan tree, while Hindu ascetics are still to be found sitting cross-legged beneath peepal trees. Peepals are just right in summer, because the slender heart-shaped leaves catch the slightest breeze and send cool currents down to the thinker below.

Personally, I prefer contemplation to meditation. I am happy to stand back from the great mulberry and study its awesome proportions. Not a tall tree, but it has an immense girth—my three-room apartment in Mussoorie would have fitted quite snugly into it. A small temple beside the tree looked very tiny indeed, and the children playing among its protruding roots could have been kittens.

As I said, I'm not one for meditating beneath trees, but that's really because something always happens to me when I try. I don't know how the great sages managed, but I find it difficult to concentrate when a Rhesus monkey comes up to me and stares me in the face. Or when a horse-chestnut bounces off my head. Or when a cloud of pollen slides off the branch of a deodar and down the back of my shirt. Or when a woodpecker starts hammering away a few feet up the trunk from where I sit. I expect the great ones were immune to all this arboreal activity. I'm just a nature-lover, easily distracted by the caterpillar crawling up my leg.

And so I am happy to stand back and admire the 'good, green-hatted people', as a visitor from another planet described the trees in a story by R.L. Stevenson. Especially the old trees. They have seen a lot of odd humans coming and going, and they know I'm just a seventy-year-old boy without any pretensions to being a sage.

# The Wind on Haunted Hill

Whoo, whoo, whoo, cried the wind as it swept down from the Himalayan snows. It hurried over the hills and passes and hummed and moaned through the tall pines and deodars. There was little on Haunted Hill to stop the wind-only a few stunted trees and bushes and the ruins of a small settlement.

On the slopes of the next hill was a village. People kept large stones on their tin roofs to prevent them from being blown off. There was nearly always a strong wind in these parts. Three children were spreading clothes out to dry on a low stone wall, putting a stone on each piece.

Eleven-year-old Usha, dark-haired and rose-cheeked, struggled with her grandfather's long, loose shirt. Her younger brother, Suresh, was doing his best to hold down a bedsheet, while Usha's friend, Binya, a slightly older girl, helped.

Once everything was firmly held down by stones, they climbed up on the flat rocks and sat there sunbathing and staring across the fields at the ruins on Haunted Hill.

'I must go to the bazaar today,' said Usha.

'I wish I could come too,' said Binya. 'But I have to help with the cows.'

'I can come!' said eight-year-old Suresh. He was always ready to visit the bazaar, which was three miles away, on the other side of the hill.

'No, you can't,' said Usha. 'You must help Grandfather chop wood.'

'Won't you feel scared returning alone?' he asked. 'There are ghosts on Haunted Hill!'

'I'll be back before dark. Ghosts don't appear during the day.'

'Are there lots of ghosts in the ruins?' asked Binya.

'Grandfather says so. He says that over a hundred years ago, some Britishers lived on the hill. But the settlement was always being struck by lightning, so they moved away.'

'But if they left, why is the place visited by ghosts?'

'Because, Grandfather says, during a terrible storm, one of the houses was hit by lightning, and everyone in it was killed. Even the children.'

'How many children?'

'Two. A boy and his sister. Grandfather saw them playing there in the moonlight.'

'Wasn't he frightened?'

'No. Old people don't mind ghosts.'

Usha set out for the bazaar at two in the afternoon. It was about an hour's walk. The path went through yellow fields of flowering mustard, then along the saddle of the hill, and up, straight through the ruins. Usha had often gone that way to shop at the bazaar or to see her aunt, who lived in the town nearby.

Wild flowers bloomed on the crumbling walls of the ruins, and a wild plum tree grew straight out of the floor of what had once been a hall. It was covered with soft, white blossoms. Lizards scuttled over the stones, while a whistling thrush, its deep purple plumage glistening in the sunshine, sat on a window-sill and sang its heart out.

Usha sang too, as she skipped lightly along the path, which clipped steeply down to the valley and led to the little town with its quaint bazaar.

Moving leisurely, Usha bought spices, sugar and matches. With the two rupees she had saved from her pocket-money, she chose a necklace of amber-coloured beads for herself and some marbles for Suresh. Then she had her mother's slippers repaired at a cobbler's shop.

Finally, Usha went to visit Aunt Lakshmi at her flat above the shops. They were talking and drinking cups of hot, sweet tea when Usha realized that dark clouds had gathered over the mountains. She quickly picked up her things, said good-bye to her aunt, and set out for the village.

Strangely, the wind had dropped. The trees were still, the crickets silent. The crows flew round in circles, then settled in an oak tree.

'I must get home before dark,' thought Usha, hurrying along the path.

But the sky had darkened and a deep rumble echoed over the hills. Usha felt the first heavy drop of rain hit her cheek. Holding the shopping bag close to her body, she quickened her pace until she was almost running. The raindrops were coming down faster now-cold, stinging pellets of rain. A flash of lightning sharply outlined the ruins on the hill, and then all was dark again. Night had fallen.

'I'll have to shelter in the ruins,' Usha thought and began to run. Suddenly the wind sprang up again, but she did not have to fight it. It was behind her now, helping her along, up the steep path and on to the brow of the hill. There was another flash of lightning, followed by a peal of thunder. The ruins loomed before her, grim and forbidding.

Usha remembered part of an old roof that would give some shelter. It would be better than trying to go on. In the dark, with the howling wind, she might stray off the path and fall over the edge of the cliff.

Whoo, whoo, whoo, howled the wind. Usha saw the wild plum tree swaying, its foliage thrashing against the ground. She found her way into the ruins, helped by the constant flicker of lightning. Usha placed her hands flat against a stone wall and moved sideways, hoping to reach the sheltered corner. Suddenly, her hand touched something soft and furry, and she gave a startled cry. Her cry was answered by another—half snarl, half screech—as something leapt away in the darkness.

With a sigh of relief Usha realized that it was the cat that lived in the ruins. For a moment she had been frightened, but now she moved quickly along the wall until she heard the rain drumming on a remnant of a tin roof. Crouched in a corner, she found some shelter. But the tin sheet groaned and clattered as if it would sail away any moment.

Usha remembered that across this empty room stood an old fireplace. Perhaps it would be drier there under the blocked chimney. But she would not attempt to find it just now—she might lose her way altogether.

Her clothes were soaked and water streamed down from her hair, forming a puddle at her feet. She thought she heard a faint cry—the cat again, or an owl? Then the storm blotted out all other sounds.

There had been no time to think of ghosts, but now that she was settled in one place, Usha remembered Grandfather's story about the lightning-blasted ruins. She hoped and prayed that lightning would not strike her.

Thunder boomed over the hills, and the lightning came quicker now. Then there was a bigger flash, and for a moment the entire ruin was lit up. A streak of blue sizzled along the floor of the building. Usha was staring straight ahead, and, as the opposite wall lit up, she saw, crouching in front of the unused fireplace, two small figures—children!

The ghostly figures seemed to look up and stare back at Usha. And then everything was dark again.

Usha's heart was in her mouth. She had seen without doubt, two ghosts on the other side of the room. She wasn't going to remain in the ruins one minute longer.

She ran towards the big gap in the wall through which she had entered. She was halfway across the open space when something—someone—fell against her. Usha stumbled, got up, and again bumped into something. She gave a frightened scream. Someone else screamed. And then there was a shout, a boy's shout, and Usha instantly recognized the voice.

'Suresh!'

'Usha!'

'Binya!'

They fell into each other's arms, so surprised and relieved that all they could do was laugh and giggle and repeat each other's names.

Then Usha said, 'I thought you were ghosts.'

'We thought you were a ghost,' said Suresh.

'Come back under the roof,' said Usha.

They huddled together in the corner, chattering with excitement and relief.

'When it grew dark, we came looking for you,' said Binya. 'And then the storm broke.'

'Shall we run back together?' asked Usha. 'I don't want to stay here any longer.'

'We'll have to wait,' said Binya. 'The path has fallen away at one place. It won't be safe in the dark, in all this rain.'

'We'll have to wait till morning,' said Suresh, 'and I'm so hungry!'

The storm continued, but they were not afraid now. They gave each other warmth and confidence. Even the ruins did not seem so forbidding.

After an hour the rain stopped, and the thunder grew more distant.

Towards dawn the whistling thrush began to sing. Its sweet, broken notes flooded the ruins with music. As the sky grew lighter, they saw that the plum tree stood upright again, though it had lost all its blossoms.

'Let's go,' said Usha.

Outside the ruins, walking along the brow of the hill, they watched the sky grow pink. When they were some distance away, Usha looked back and said, 'Can you see something behind the wall? It's like a hand waving.'

'It's just the top of the plum tree,' said Binya.

'Good-bye, good-bye...' They heard voices.

'Who said 'good-bye'?' asked Usha.

'Not I,' said Suresh.

'Not I,' said Binya.

'I heard someone calling,' said Usha.

'It's only the wind,' assured Binya.

Usha looked back at the ruins. The sun had come up and was touching the top of the wall.

'Come on,' said Suresh. 'I'm hungry.'

They hurried along the path to the village.

'Good-bye, good-bye...' Usha heard them calling. Was it just the wind?

# The Night the Roof Blew Off

We are used to sudden storms up here on the first range of the Himalayas. The old building in which we live has, for more than a hundred years, received the full force of the wind as it sweeps across the hills from the east.

We'd lived in the building for more than ten years without a disaster. It had even taken the shock of a severe earthquake. As my granddaughter Dolly said, 'It's difficult to tell the new cracks from the old!'

It's a two-storey building, and I live on the upper floor with my family: my three grandchildren and their parents. The roof is made of corrugated tin sheets, the ceiling of wooden boards. That's the traditional Mussoorie roof.

Looking back at the experience, it was the sort of thing that should have happened in a James Thurber story, like the dam that burst or the ghost who got in. But I wasn't thinking of Thurber at the time, although a few of his books were among the many I was trying to save from the icy rain pouring into my bedroom.

Our roof had held fast in many a storm, but the wind that night was really fierce. It came rushing at us with a high-pitched, eerie wail. The old roof groaned and protested. It took a battering for several hours while the rain lashed against the windows and the lights kept coming and going.

There was no question of sleeping, but we remained in bed for warmth and comfort. The fire had long since gone out as the chimney had collapsed, bringing down a shower of sooty rainwater.

After about four hours of buffeting, the roof could take it no longer. My bedroom faces east, so my portion of the roof was the first to go.

The wind got under it and kept pushing until, with a ripping, groaning sound, the metal sheets shifted and slid off the rafters, some of them dropping with claps like thunder on to the road below.

So that's it, I thought. Nothing worse can happen. As long as the ceiling stays on, I'm not getting out of bed. We'll collect our roof in the morning.

Icy water splashing down on my face made me change my mind in a hurry. Leaping from the bed, I found that much of the ceiling had gone, too. Water was pouring on my open typewriter as well as on the bedside radio and bed cover.

Picking up my precious typewriter (my companion for forty years) I stumbled into the front sitting room (and library), only to find a similar situation there. Water was pouring through the slats of the wooden ceiling, raining down on the open bookshelves.

By now I had been joined by the children, who had come to my rescue. Their section of the roof hadn't gone as yet. Their parents were struggling to close a window against the driving rain.

'Save the books!' shouted Dolly, the youngest, and that became our rallying cry for the next hour or two.

Dolly and her brother Mukesh picked up armfuls of books and carried them into their room. But the floor was awash, so the books had to be piled on their beds. Dolly was helping me gather some of my papers when a large field rat jumped on to the desk in front of her. Dolly squealed and ran for the door.

'It's all right,' said Mukesh, whose love of animals extends even to field rats. 'It's only sheltering from the storm.'

Big brother Rakesh whistled for our dog, Tony, but Tony wasn't interested in rats just then. He had taken shelter in the kitchen, the only dry spot in the house.

Two rooms were now practically roofless, and we could see the sky lit up by flashes of lightning.

There were fireworks indoors, too, as water spluttered and crackled along a damaged wire. Then the lights went out altogether.

Rakesh, at his best in an emergency, had already lit two kerosene lamps. And by their light we continued to transfer books, papers, and clothes to the children's room.

We noticed that the water on the floor was beginning to subside a little.

'Where is it going?' asked Dolly.

'Through the floor,' said Mukesh. 'Down to the flat below!'

Cries of concern from our downstairs neighbours told us

that they were having their share of the flood.

Our feet were freezing because there hadn't been time to put on proper footwear. And besides, shoes and slippers were awash by now. All chairs and tables were piled high with books. I hadn't realized the extent of my library until that night!

The available beds were pushed into the driest corner of the children's room, and there, huddled in blankets and quilts, we spent the remaining hours of the night while the storm continued.

Towards morning the wind fell, and it began to snow. Through the door to the sitting room I could see snowflakes drifting through the gaps in the ceiling, settling on picture frames. Ordinary things like a glue bottle and a small clock took on a certain beauty when covered with soft snow.

Most of us dozed off.

When dawn came, we found the windowpanes encrusted with snow and icicles. The rising sun struck through the gaps in the ceiling and turned everything golden. Snow crystals glistened on the empty bookshelves. But the books had been saved.

Rakesh went out to find a carpenter and tinsmith, while the rest of us started putting things in the sun to dry. By evening, we'd put much of the roof back on.

It's a much-improved roof now, and we look forward to the next storm with confidence!

# The Last Truck Ride

*[Twice a day Pritam Singh takes his battered, old truck on
the narrow, mountainous roads, to the limestone quarry. He
is in the habit of driving fast. The brakes of his truck are in
good condition. What happens when a stray mule suddenly
appears on the road?]*

A horn blared, shattering the silence of the mountains, and
a truck came round the bend in the road. A herd of goats
scattered to left and right.

The goat-herds cursed as a cloud of dust enveloped them,
and then the truck had left them behind and was rattling along
the stony, unpaved hill road.

At the wheel of the truck, stroking his gray moustache, sat
Pritam Singh, a turbaned Sikh. It was his own truck. He did not
allow anyone else to drive it. Everyday he made two trips to
the limestone quarries, carrying truckloads of limestone back

to the depot at the bottom of the hill. He was paid by the trip, and he was always anxious to get in two trips everyday.

Sitting beside him was Nathu, his cleaner-boy. Nathu was a sturdy boy, with a round cheerful face. It was difficult to guess his age. He might have been twelve or he might have been fifteen—he did not know himself, since no one in his village had troubled to record his birthday—but the hard life he led probably made him look older than his years. He belonged to the hills, but his village was far away, on the next range.

Last year the potato crop had failed. As a result there was no money for salt, sugar, soap and flour, and Nathu's parents, and small brothers and sisters couldn't live entirely on the onions and artichokes which were about the only crops that had survived the drought. There had been no rain that summer. So Nathu waved good-bye to his people and came down to the town in the valley to look for work. Someone directed him to the limestone depot. He was too young to work at the quarries, breaking stones and loading them on the trucks; but Pritam Singh, one of the older drivers, was looking for someone to clean and look after his truck. Nathu looked like a bright, strong boy, and he was taken on at ten rupees a day.

That had been six months ago, and now Nathu was an experienced hand at looking after trucks, riding in them and even sleeping in them. He got on well with Pritam Singh, the grizzled, fifty-year-old Sikh, who had well-to-do sons in Punjab, but whose sturdy independence kept him on the road in his battered old truck.

Pritam Singh pressed hard on his horn. Now there was no one on the road—no animals, no humans—but Pritam was fond of his horn and liked blowing it. It was music to his ears.

'One more year on this road,' said Pritam. 'Then I'll sell my truck and retire.'

'Who will buy this truck? said Nathu. 'It will retire before you do.' 'Don't be cheeky, boy. She's only twenty-years-old. There are still a few years left in her!' And as though to prove it, he blew his horn again. Its strident sound echoed and re-echoed down the mountain gorge. A pair of wild fowl, disturbed by the noise, flew out from the bushes and glided across the road in front of the truck.

Pritam Singh's thoughts went to his dinner.

'Haven't had a good meal for *days,*' he grumbled.

'Haven't had a good meal for weeks,' said Nathu, although he looked quite well-fed.

'Tomorrow I'll give you dinner,' said Pritam. 'Tandoori chicken and pilaf rice.'

'I'll believe it when I see it,' said Nathu.

Pritam Singh sounded his horn again before slowing down. The road had become narrow and precipitous, and trotting ahead of them was a train of mules. As the horn blared, one mule ran forward, one ran backwards. One went uphill, one went downhill. Soon there were mules all over the place.

'You can never tell with mules,' said Pritam, after he had left them behind.

The hills were bare and dry. Much of the forest had long since disappeared. Just a few scraggy old oaks still grew on the steep hillside. This particular range was rich in limestone, and the hills were scarred by quarrying.

'Are your hills as bare as these?' asked Pritam.

'No, they have not started blasting there as yet,' said Nathu.

'We still have a few trees. And there is a walnut tree in front of our house, which gives us two baskets of walnuts every year'.

'And do you have water?'

'There is a stream at the bottom of the hill. But for the fields, we have to depend on the rainfall. And there was no rain last year.'

'It will rain soon,' said Pritam. 'I can smell rain. It is coming from the north.'

'It will settle the dust.'

The dust was everywhere. The truck was full of it. The leaves of the shrubs and the few trees were thick with it. Nathu could feel the dust near his eyelids and on his lips. As they approached the quarries, the dust increased—but it was a different kind of dust now—whiter, stinging the eyes, irritating the nostrils—limestone dust, hanging in the air.

The blasting was in progress.

Pritam Singh brought the truck to a halt. 'Let's wait a bit,' he said.

They sat in silence, staring through the windscreen at the scarred cliffs about a hundred yards down the road. There was no sign of life around them.

Suddenly, the hillside blossomed outwards, followed by a sharp crack of explosives. Earth and rock hurtled down the hillside.

Nathu watched in awe as shrubs and small trees were flung into the air. It always frightened him not so much the sight of the rocks bursting asunder, but the trees being flung aside and destroyed. He thought of his own trees at home—the walnut, the pines—and wondered if one day they would suffer the same fate, and whether the mountains would all become a desert like this particular range. No trees, no grass, no water—only the choking dust of the limestone quarries.

Pritam Singh pressed hard on his horn again, to let the people at the site know he was coming. Soon they were parked outside a small shed, where the contractor and the overseer were sipping cups of tea. A short distance away some labourers were hammering at chunks of rock, breaking them up into manageable blocks. A pile of stones stood ready for loading, while the rock that had just been blasted lay scattered about the hillside.

'Come and have a cup of tea,' called out the contractor.

'Get on with the loading,' said Pritam. 'I can't hang about all afternoon. There's another trip to make and it gets dark early these days.'

But he sat down on a bench and ordered two cups of tea from the stall-owner. The overseer strolled over to the group of labourers and told them to start loading. Nathu let down the grid at the back of the truck.

Nathu stood back while the men loaded the truck with limestone rocks. He was glad that he was chubby: thin people seemed to feel the cold much more—like the contractor, a skinny fellow who was shivering in his expensive overcoat.

To keep himself warm, Nathu began helping the labourers with the loading.

'Don't expect to be paid for that,' said the contractor, for whom every extra paise spent was a paisa off his profits.

'Don't worry,' said Nadhu, 'I don't work for contractors. I

work for Pritam Singh.'

'That's right,' called out Pritam. 'And mind what you say to Nathu—he's nobody's servant!'

It took them almost an hour to fill the truck with stones. The contractor wasn't happy until there was no space left for a single stone. Then four of the six labourers climbed on the pile of stones. They would ride back to the depot on the truck. The contractor, his overseer, and the others would follow by jeep. 'Let's go!' said Pritam, getting behind the steering wheel. 'I want to be back here and then home by eight o'clock. I'm going to a marriage party tonight!'

Nathu jumped in beside him, banging his door shut. It never opened at a touch. Pritam always joked that his truck was held together with Sellotape.

He was in good spirits. He started his engine, blew his horn, and burst into a song as the truck started out on the return journey.

The labourers were singing too, as the truck swung round the sharp bends of the winding mountain road. Nathu was feeling quite dizzy. The door beside him rattled on its hinges.

'Not so fast,' he said.

'Oh,' said Pritam, 'And since when did you become nervous about fast driving?'

'Since today,' said Nathu.

'And what's wrong with today?'

'I don't know. It's just that kind of day, I suppose.'

'You are getting old,' said Pritam. 'That's your trouble.'

'Just wait till you get to be my age,' said Nathu.

'No more cheek,' said Pritam, and stepped on the accelerator and drove faster. As they swung round a bend, Nathu looked out of his window. All he saw was the sky above and the valley below. They were very near the edge. But it was always like that on this narrow road. After a few more hairpin bends, the road started descending steeply to the valley.

'I'll just test the brakes,' said Pritam and jammed down on there so suddenly that one of the labourers almost fell off at the back.

They called out in protest.

'Hang on!' shouted Pritarn.

'You're nearly home!'

'Don't try any short cuts,' said Nathu.

Just then a stray mule appeared in the middle of the road. Pritam swung the steering wheel over to his right; but the road turned left, and the truck went straight over the edge.

As it tipped over, hanging for a few seconds on the edge of the cliff, the labourers leapt from the back of the truck.

'The truck pitched forward, bouncing over the rocks, turning over on its side and rolling over twice before coming to rest against the trunk of a scraggy old oak tree. Had it missed the tree, the truck would have plunged a few hundred feet down to the bottom of the gorge.

Two labourers sat on the hillside, stunned and badly shaken.

The other two had picked themselves up and were running back to the quarry for help.

Nathu had landed in a bed of nettles. He was smarting all over, but he wasn't really hurt.

His first impulse was to get up and run back with the labourers. Then he realized that Pritam was still in the truck.

If he wasn't dead, he would certainly be badly injured.

Nathu skidded down the steep slope, calling out, 'Pritam, Pritam, are you all right?'

There was no answer.

Then he saw Pritam's arm and half his body jutting out of the open door of the truck. It was a strange position to be in, half in and half out. When Nathu came nearer, he saw Pritam was jammed in the driver's seat, held there by the steering wheel which was pressed hard against his chest. Nathu thought he was dead. But as he was about to turn away and clamber back up the hill, he saw Pritam open one blackened swollen eye. It looked straight up at Nathu.

'Are you alive?' whispered Nathu, terrified.

'What do you think?' muttered Pritam. He closed his eye again.

When the contractor and his men arrived, it took them almost an hour to get him to a hospital in the town. He had a broken collarbone, a dislocated shoulder, and several fractured ribs. But the doctors said he was repairable- which was more than could be said for his truck.

'The truck's finished,' said Pritam, when Nathu came to see him a few days later. 'Now 'I'll have to go home and live with my sons. But you can get work on another truck.'

'No,' said Nathu. 'I'm gong home too.'

'And what will you do there?'

'I'll work on the land. It's better to grow things on the land than to blast things out of it.'

They were silent for some time.

'Do you know something?' said Pritam finally. 'But for that

tree, the truck would have ended up at the bottom of the hill and I wouldn't be here, all bandaged up and talking to you. It was the tree that saved me. Remember that, boy.'

'I'll remember,' said Nathu.

# And Now We Are Twelve

People often ask me why I've chosen to live in Mussoori for so long—almost forty years without any significant breaks.

'I forgot to go away,' I tell them, but of course, that isn't the real reason.

The people here are friendly, but then people are friendly in a great many other places. The hills, the valleys are beautiful; but they are just as beautiful in Kulu or Kumaon.

'This is where the family has grown up and where we all live,' I say, and those who don't know me are puzzled because the general impression of the writer is of a reclusive old bachelor.

Unmarried I may be, but single I am not. Not since Prem came to live and work with me in 1970. A year later, he was married. Then his children came along and stole my heart; and when they grew up, their children came along and stole my wits. So now I'm an enchanted bachelor, head of a family of twelve. Sometimes I go out to bat, sometimes to bowl, but generally I prefer to be twelfth man, carrying out the drinks!

In the old days, when I was a solitary writer living on baked beans, the prospect of my suffering from obesity was very remote. Now there is a little more of author than there used to be, and the other day five-year-old Gautam patted me on my tummy (or balcony, as I prefer to call it) and remarked: 'Dada, you should join the WWE.'

'I'm already a member,' I said, 'I joined the World Wildlife Fund years ago.'

'Not that,' he said. 'I mean the World Wrestling Federation.'

If I have a tummy today, it's thanks to Gautam's grandfather and now his mother who, over the years, have made sure that I am well-fed and well-proportioned.

Forty years ago, when I was a lean young man, people would look at me and say, 'Poor chap, he's definitely undernourished. What on earth made him take up writing as a profession?' Now they look at me and say, 'You wouldn't think he was a writer, would you? Too well nourished!'

◆

It was a cold, wet and windy March evening when Prem came back from the village with his wife and first-born child, then just four months old. In those days, they had to walk to the house from the bus stand; it was a half hour walk in the cold rain, and the baby was all wrapped up when they entered the front room. Finally, I got a glimpse of him, and he of mne, and it was friendship at first sight. Little Rakesh (as he was to be called) grabbed me by the nose and held on. He did not have much of a nose to grab, but he had a dimpled chin and I played with it until he smiled.

The little chap spent a good deal of his time with me during those first two years of his in Maplewood—learning to crawl, to toddle, and then to walk unsteadily about the little sitting-room. I would carry him into the garden, and later, up the steep gravel path to the main road. Rakesh enjoyed these little excursions, and so did I, because in pointing out trees, flowers, birds, butterflies, beetles, grasshoppers, et al, I was giving myself a chance to observe them better instead of just taking them for granted.

In particular, there was a pair of squirrels that lived in the big oak tree outside the cottage. Squirrels are rare in Mussoorie though common enough down in the valley. This couple must have come up for the summer. They became quite friendly, and although they never got around to taking food from our hands, they were soon entering the house quite freely. The sitting room window opened directly on to the oak tree whose various denizens—ranging from stag-beetles to small birds and even an acrobatic bat—took to darting in and out of the cottage at various times of the day or night.

Life at Maplewood was quite idyllic, and when Rakesh's baby brother, Suresh, came into the world, it seemed we were all set for a long period of domestic bliss; but at such times tragedy is often lurking just around the corner. Suresh was just over a year old when he contracted tetanus. Doctors and hospitals were of no avail. He suffered—as any child would from this terrible affliction—and left this world before he had a chance of getting to know it. His parents were broken-hearted. And I feared for Rakesh, for he wasn't a very healthy boy, and two of his cousins in the village had already succumbed to tuberculosis.

It was to be a difficult year for me. A criminal charge was brought against me for a slightly risque story I'd written for a Bombay magazine. I had to face trial in Bombay and this involved three journeys there over a period of a year and a half, before an irate but perceptive judge found the charges baseless and gave me an honourable acquittal.

It's the only time I've been involved with the law and I sincerely hope it is the last. Most cases drag on interminably, and the main beneficiaries are the lawyers. My trial would have been much longer had not the prosecutor died of a heart attack in the middle of the proceedings. His successor did not pursue it with the same vigour. His heart was not in it. The whole issue had started with a complaint by a local politician, and when he lost interest so did the prosecution. Nevertheless the trial, once begun, had to be seen through. The defence (organized by the concerned magazine) marshalled its witnesses (which included Nissim Ezekiel and the Marathi playwright Vijay Tendulkar). I made a short speech which couldn't have been very memorable as I have forgotten it! And everyone, including the judge, was bored with the whole business. After that, I steered clear of controversial publications. I have never set out to shock the world. Telling a meaningful story was all that really mattered. And that is still the case.

I was looking forward to continuing our idyllic existence in Maplewood, but it was not to be. The powers-that-be, in the shape of the Public Works Department (PWD), had decided to build a 'strategic' road just below the cottage and without any warning to us, all the trees in the vicinity were felled (including the friendly old oak) and the hillside was rocked by explosives and bludgeoned by bulldozers. I decided it was time to move. Prem and Chandra (Rakesh's mother) wanted to move too; not because of the road, but because they associated the house with the death of little Suresh, whose presence seemed to haunt every room, every corner of the cottage. His little cries of pain and suffering still echoed through the still hours of the night.

I rented rooms at the top of Landour, a good thousand feet higher up the mountain. Rakesh was now old enough to go to school, and every morning I would walk with him down to the little convent school near the clock tower. Prem would go to fetch him in the afternoon. The walk took us about half an hour, and on the way Rakesh would ask for a story and I would have to rack my brains in order to invent one. I am not the most inventive of writers, and fantastical plots are beyond me. My forte is observation, recollection, and reflection. Small boys prefer action. So I invented a leopard who suffered from acute indigestion because he'd eaten one human too many and a belt buckle was causing an obstruction.

This went down quite well until Rakesh asked me how the leopard got around the problem of the victim's clothes.

'The secret,' I said, 'is to pounce on them when their trousers are off!'

Not the stuff of which great picture books are made, but then, I've never attempted to write stories for beginners. Red Riding Hood's granny-eating wolf always scared me as a small boy, and yet parents have always found it acceptable for toddlers. Possibly they feel grannies are expendable.

Mukesh was born around this time and Savitri (Dolly) a couple of years later. When Dolly grew older, she was annoyed at having been named Savitri (my choice), which is now considered very old fashioned; so we settled for Dolly. I can understand a child's dissatisfaction with given names. My first name was Owen, which in Welsh means 'brave'. As I am not in the least brave, I have preferred not to use it. One given name and one surname should be enough.

When my granny said, 'But you should try to be brave, otherwise how will you survive in this cruel world?' I replied:

'Don't worry, I can run very fast.'

Not that I've ever had to do much running, except when I was pursued by a lissome Australian lady who thought I'd make a good obedient husband. It wasn't so much the lady I was running from, but the prospect of spending the rest of my life in some remote cattle station in the Australian outback. Anyone who has tried to drag me away from India has always met with stout resistance.

◆

Up on the heights of Landour lived a motley crowd. My immediate neighbours included a Frenchwoman who played the sitar (very badly) all through the night; a Spanish lady with two husbands. One of whom practised acupuncture—rather ineffectively as far as he was concerned, for he seemed to be dying of some mysterious debilitating disease. The other came and went rather mysteriously, and finally ended up in Tihar Jail, having been apprehended at Delhi airport carrying a large amount of contraband hashish.

Apart from these and a few other colourful characters, the area was inhabited by some very respectable people, retired brigadiers, air marshals and rear admirals, almost all of whom were busy writing their memoirs. I had to read or listen to extracts from their literary efforts. This was slow torture. A few years before, I had done a stint of editing for a magazine called *Imprint*. It had involved going through hundreds of badly written manuscripts, and in some cases (friends of the owner!) re-writing some of them for publication. One of life's joys had been to throw up that particular job, and now here I was, besieged by all the top brass of the Army, Navy and Air Force, each one determined that I should read, inwardly digest, improve, and if possible find a publisher for their outpourings. Thank goodness they were all retired. I could not be shot or court-martialled. But at least two of them set their wives upon me, and these intrepid ladies would turn up around noon with my 'homework'—typescripts to read and edit! There was no escape. My own writing was of no consequence to them. I told them that I was taking sitar lessons, but they disapproved, saying I was more suited to the tabla.

When Prem discovered a set of vacant rooms further down the Landour slope, close to school and bazaar, I rented them without hesitation. This was Ivy Cottage. Come up and see me sometimes, but leave your manuscripts behind.

When we came to Ivy Cottage in 1980, we were six, Dolly having just been born. Now, twenty-four years later, we are twelve. I think that's a reasonable expansion. The increase has been brought about by Rakesh's marriage twelve years ago, and Mukesh's marriage two years ago. Both precipitated themselves into marriage when they were barely twenty, and both were lucky. Beena and Binita, who happen to be real sisters, have brightened and enlivened our lives with their happy, positive natures and the wonderful children they have brought into the world. More about them later.

Ivy Cottage has, on the whole, been kind to us, and particularly kind to me. Some houses like their occupants, others don't. Maplewood, set in the shadow of the hill lacked a natural cheerfulness; there was a settled gloom about the place. The house at the top of Landour was too exposed to the elements to have any sort of character. The wind moaning in the deodars may have inspired the sitar player but it did nothing for my writing. I produced very little up there. On the other hand, Ivy Cottage—especially my little room facing the sunrise— has been conducive to creative work. Novellas, poems, essays, children's stories, anthologies, have all come tumbling on to whatever sheets of paper happen to be nearest me. As I write by hand, I have only to grab for the nearest pad, loose sheet, page-proof or envelope whenever the muse takes hold of me; which is surprisingly often.

I came here when I was nearing fifty. Now I'm seventy, and instead of drying up, as some writers do in their later years, I find myself writing with as much ease and assurance as when I was twenty. And I enjoy writing. It's not a burdensome task. I may not have anything of earth-shattering significance to convey to the world, but in conveying my sentiments to you, dear readers, and in telling you something about my relationship with people and the natural world, I hope to bring a little pleasure and sunshine into your life.

Life isn't a bed of roses, not for any of us, and I have never had the comforts or luxuries that wealth can provide. But here

I am, doing my own thing, in my own time and my own way. What more can I ask of life? Give me a big cash prize and I'd still be here. I happen to like the view from my window. And I like to have Gautam coming up to me, patting me on the tummy, and telling me that I'll make a good goalkeeper one day.

It's a Sunday morning, as I come to the conclusion of this chapter. There's bedlam in the house. Siddharth's football keeps smashing against the front door. Shrishti is practising her dance routine in the back verandah. Gautam has cut his finger and is trying his best to bandage it with cellotape. He is, of course, the youngest of Rakesh's three musketeers, and probably the most independent-minded. Siddharth, now ten, is restless, never quite able to expend all his energy. 'Does not pay enough attention,' says his teacher. It must be hard for anyone to pay attention in a class of sixty! How does the poor teacher pay attention?

If you, dear reader, have any ambitions to be a writer, you must first rid yourself of any notion that perfect peace and quiet is the first requirement. There is no such thing as perfect peace and quiet except perhaps in a monastery or a cave in the mountains. And what would you write about, living in a cave? One should be able to write in a train, a bus, a bullockcart, in good weather or bad, on a park bench or in the middle of a noisy classroom.

Of course, the best place is the sun-drenched desk right next to my bed. It isn't always sunny here, but on a good day like this, it's ideal. The children are getting ready for school, dogs are barking in the street, and down near the water tap there's an altercation between two women with empty buckets, the tap having dried up. But these are all background noises and will subside in due course. They are not directed at me.

Hello! Here's Atish, Mukesh's little ten-month old infant, crawling over the rug, curious to know why I'm sitting on the edge of my bed scribbling away, when I should be playing with him. So I shall play with him for five minutes and then come back to this page. Giving him my time is important. After all, I won't be around when he grows up.

Half-an-hour later. Atish soon tired of playing with me, but meanwhile Gautam had absconded with my pen. When I asked him to return it, he asked, 'Why don't you get a computer? Then we can play games on it.'

'My pen is faster than any computer,' I tell him, 'I wrote three pages this morning without getting out of bed. And yesterday I wrote two pages sitting under Billoo's chestnut tree.'

'Until a chestnut fell on your head,' says Gautam, 'Did it hurt?'

'Only a little,' I said, putting on a brave front.

He had saved the chestnut and now he showed it to me. The smooth brown horse-chestnut shone in the sunlight.

'Let's stick it in the ground,' I said. 'Then in the spring a chestnut tree will come up.'

So we went outside and planted the chestnut on a plot of wasteland. Hopefully a small tree will burst through the earth at about the time this little book is published.

# The School among the Pines

## 1

A leopard, lithe and sinewy, drank at the mountain stream, and then lay down on the grass to bask in the late February sunshine. Its tail twitched occasionally and the animal appeared to be sleeping. At the sound of distant voices it raised its head to listen, then stood up and leapt lightly over the boulders in the stream, disappearing among the trees on the opposite bank.

A minute or two later, three children came walking down the forest path. They were a girl and two boys, and they were singing in their local dialect an old song they had learnt from their grandparents.

> *Five more miles to go!*
> *We climb through rain and snow.*
> *A river to cross...*
> *A mountain to pass...*
> *Now we've four more miles to go!*

Their school satchels looked new, their clothes had been washed and pressed. Their loud and cheerful singing startled a Spotted Forktail. The bird left its favourite rock in the stream and flew down the dark ravine.

'Well, we have only three more miles to go,' said the bigger boy, Prakash, who had been this way hundreds of times. 'But first we have to cross the stream.'

He was a sturdy twelve-year-old with eyes like raspberries and a mop of bushy hair that refused to settle down on his head. The girl and her small brother were taking this path for the first time.

'I'm feeling tired, Bina,' said the little boy.

Bina smiled at him, and Prakash said, 'Don't worry, Sonu, you'll get used to the walk. There's plenty of time.' He glanced at the old watch he'd been given by his grandfather. It needed constant winding. 'We can rest here for five or six minutes.'

They sat down on a smooth boulder and watched the clear water of the shallow stream tumbling downhill. Bina examined the old watch on Prakash's wrist. The glass was badly scratched and she could barely make out the figures on the dial. 'Are you sure it still gives the right time?' she asked.

'Well, it loses five minutes every day, so I put it ten minutes forward at night. That means by morning it's quite accurate! Even our teacher, Mr Mani, asks me for the time. If he doesn't ask, I tell him! The clock in our classroom keeps stopping.'

They removed their shoes and let the cold mountain water run over their feet. Bina was the same age as Prakash. She had pink cheeks, soft brown eyes, and hair that was just beginning to lose its natural curls. Hers was a gentle face, but a determined little chin showed that she could be a strong person. Sonu, her younger brother, was ten. He was a thin boy who had been sickly as a child but was now beginning to fill out. Although he did not look very athletic, he could run like the wind.

Bina had been going to school in her own village of Koli, on the other side of the mountain. But it had been a primary school, finishing at Class Five. Now, in order to study in the Sixth, she would have to walk several miles every day to Nauti, where there was a high school going up to the Eighth. It had been decided that Sonu would also shift to the new school, to give Bina company. Prakash, their neighbour in Koli, was already a pupil at the Nauti school. His mischievous nature, which sometimes got him into trouble, had resulted in his having to repeat a year.

But this didn't seem to bother him. 'What's the hurry?' he had told his indignant parents. 'You're not sending me to a foreign land when I finish school. And our cows aren't running away, are they?'

'You would prefer to look after the cows, wouldn't you?' asked Bina, as they got up to continue their walk.

'Oh, school's all right. Wait till you see old Mr Mani. He always gets our names mixed up, as well as the subjects he's supposed to be teaching. At out last lesson, instead of maths, he gave us a geography lesson!'

'More fun than maths,' said Bina.

'Yes, but there's a new teacher this year. She's very young, they say, just out of college. I wonder what she'll be like.'

Bina walked faster and Sonu had some trouble keeping

up with them. She was excited about the new school and the prospect of different surroundings. She had seldom been outside her own village, with its small school and single ration shop. The day's routine never varied—helping her mother in the fields or with household tasks like fetching water from the spring or cutting grass and fodder for the cattle. Her father, who was a soldier, was away for nine months in the year and Sonu was still too small for the heavier tasks.

As they neared Nauti village, they were joined by other children coming from different directions. Even where there were no major roads, the mountains were full of little lanes and short cuts. Like a game of snakes and ladders, these narrow paths zigzagged around the hills and villages, cutting through fields and crossing narrow ravines until they came together to form a fairly busy road along which mules, cattle and goats joined the throng.

Nauti was a fairly large village, and from here a broader but dustier road started for Tehri. There was a small bus, several trucks and (for part of the way) a road-roller. The road hadn't been completed because the heavy diesel roller couldn't take the steep climb to Nauti. It stood on the roadside half way up the road from Tehri.

Prakash knew almost everyone in the area, and exchanged greetings and gossip with other children as well as with muleteers, bus drivers, milkmen and labourers working on the road. He loved telling everyone the time, even if they weren't interested.

'It's nine o'clock,' he would announce, glancing at his wrist. 'Isn't your bus leaving today?'

'Off with you!' the bus driver would respond, 'I'll leave when I'm ready.'

As the children approached Nauti, the small flat school buildings came into view on the outskirts of the village, fringed with a line of long-leaved pines. A small crowd had assembled on the playing field. Something unusual seemed to have happened. Prakash ran forward to see what it was all about. Bina and Sonu stood aside, waiting in a patch of sunlight near the boundary wall.

Prakash soon came running back to them. He was bubbling over with excitement.

'It's Mr Mani!' he gasped. 'He's disappeared! People are saying a leopard must have carried him off!'

2

Mr Mani wasn't really old. He was about fifty-five and was expected to retire soon. But for the children, adults over forty seemed ancient! And Mr Mani had always been a bit absent-minded, even as a young man.

He had gone out for his early morning walk, saying he'd be back by eight o'clock, in time to have his breakfast and be ready for class. He wasn't married, but his sister and her husband stayed with him. When it was past nine o'clock his sister presumed he'd stopped at a neighbour's house for breakfast (he loved tucking into other people's breakfast) and that he had gone on to school from there. But when the school bell rang at ten o'clock, and everyone but Mr Mani was present, questions were asked and guesses were made.

No one had seen him return from his walk and enquiries

made in the village showed that he had not stopped at anyone's house. For Mr Mani to disappear was puzzling; for him to disappear without his breakfast was extraordinary.

Then a milkman returning from the next village said he had seen a leopard sitting on a rock on the outskirts of the pine forest. There had been talk of a cattle-killer in the valley, of leopards and other animals being displaced by the construction of a dam. But as yet no one had heard of a leopard attacking a man. Could Mr Mani have been its first victim? Someone found a strip of red cloth entangled in a blackberry bush and went running through the village showing it to everyone. Mr Mani had been known to wear red pyjamas. Surely, he had been seized and eaten! But where were his remains? And why had he been in his pyjamas?

Meanwhile, Bina and Sonu and the rest of the children had followed their teachers into the school playground. Feeling a little lost, Bina looked around for Prakash. She found herself facing a dark slender young woman wearing spectacles, who must have been in her early twenties—just a little too old to be another student. She had a kind expressive face and she seemed a little concerned by all that had been happening.

Bina noticed that she had lovely hands; it was obvious that the new teacher hadn't milked cows or worked in the fields!

'You must be new here,' said the teacher, smiling at Bina. 'And is this your little brother?'

'Yes, we've come from Koli village. We were at school there.'

'It's a long walk from Koli. You didn't see any leopards, did you? Well, I'm new too. Are you in the Sixth class?'

'Sonu is in the Third. I'm in the Sixth.'

'Then I'm your new teacher. My name is Tania Ramola. Come along, let's see if we can settle down in our classroom.'

Mr Mani turned up at twelve o'clock, wondering what all the fuss was about. No, he snapped, he had not been attacked by a leopard; and yes, he had lost his pyjamas and would someone kindly return them to him?

'How did you lose your pyjamas, sir?' asked Prakash.

'They were blown off the washing line!' snapped Mr Mani.

After much questioning, Mr Mani admitted that he had gone further than he had intended, and that he had lost his way coming back. He had been a bit upset because the new teacher, a slip of a girl, had been given charge of the Sixth, while he was still with the Fifth, along with that troublesome boy Prakash, who kept on reminding him of the time! The headmaster had explained that as Mr Mani was due to retire at the end of the year, the school did not wish to burden him with a senior class. But Mr Mani looked upon the whole thing as a plot to get rid of him. He glowered at Miss Ramola whenever he passed her. And when she smiled back at him, he looked the other way!

Mr Mani had been getting even more absent-minded of late—putting on his shoes without his socks, wearing his homespun waistcoat inside out, mixing up people's names and, of course, eating other people's lunches and dinners. His sister had made a special mutton broth (*pai*) for the postmaster, who was down with flu and had asked Mr Mani to take it over in a thermos. When the postmaster opened the thermos, he found only a few drops of broth at the bottom—Mr Mani had drunk the rest somewhere along the way.

When sometimes Mr Mani spoke of his coming retirement, it was to describe his plans for the small field he owned just behind the house. Right now, it was full of potatoes, which did not require much looking after; but he had plans for growing dahlias, roses, French beans, and other fruits and flowers.

The next time he visited Tehri, he promised himself, he would buy some dahlia bulbs and rose cuttings. The monsoon season would be a good time to put them down. And meanwhile, his potatoes were still flourishing.

3

Bina enjoyed her first day at the new school. She felt at ease with Miss Ramola, as did most of the boys and girls in her class. Tania Ramola had been to distant towns such as Delhi and Lucknow—places they had only read about—and it was said that she had a brother who was a pilot and flew planes all over the world. Perhaps he'd fly over Nauti some day!

Most of the children had, of course, seen planes flying overhead, but none of them had seen a ship, and only a few had been in a train. Tehri mountain was far from the railway and hundreds of miles from the sea. But they all knew about the big dam that was being built at Tehri, just forty miles away.

Bina, Sonu and Prakash had company for part of the way home, but gradually the other children went off in different directions. Once they had crossed the stream, they were on their own again.

It was a steep climb all the way back to their village. Prakash had a supply of peanuts which he shared with Bina and Sonu, and at a small spring they quenched their thirst.

When they were less than a mile from home, they met a postman who had finished his round of the villages in the area and was now returning to Nauti.

'Don't waste time along the way,' he told them. 'Try to get home before dark.'

'What's the hurry?' asked Prakash, glancing at his watch. 'It's only five o'clock.'

'There's a leopard around. I saw it this morning, not far from the stream. No one is sure how it got here. So don't take any chances. Get home early.'

'So there really is a leopard,' said Sonu.

They took his advice and walked faster, and Sonu forgot to complain about his aching feet.

They were home well before sunset.

There was a smell of cooking in the air and they were hungry.

'Cabbage and roti,' said Prakash gloomily. 'But I could eat anything today.' He stopped outside his small slate-roofed house, and Bina and Sonu waved him goodbye, then carried on across a couple of ploughed fields until they reached their small stone house.

'Stuffed tomatoes,' said Sonu, sniffing just outside the front door.

'And lemon pickle,' said Bina, who had helped cut, sun and salt the lemons a month previously.

Their mother was lighting the kitchen stove. They greeted her with great hugs and demands for an immediate dinner. She was a good cook who could make even the simplest of dishes taste delicious. Her favourite saying was, 'Homemade *pai* is better than chicken soup in Delhi,' and Bina and Sonu had to agree.

Electricity had yet to reach their village, and they took their meal by the light of a kerosene lamp. After the meal, Sonu settled down to do a little homework, while Bina stepped outside to look at the stars.

Across the fields, someone was playing a flute. 'It must be Prakash,' thought Bina. 'He always breaks off on the high notes.' But the flute music was simple and appealing, and she began singing softly to herself in the dark.

**4**

Mr Mani was having trouble with the porcupines. They had been getting into his garden at night and digging up and eating his potatoes. From his bedroom window—left open, now that the mild-April weather had arrived—he could listen to them enjoying the vegetables he had worked hard to grow. Scrunch, scrunch! *Katar, katar*, as their sharp teeth sliced through the largest and juiciest of potatoes. For Mr Mani it was as though they were biting through his own flesh. And the sound of them digging industriously as they rooted up those healthy, leafy plants, made him tremble with rage and indignation. The unfairness of it all!

Yes, Mr Mani hated porcupines. He prayed for their destruction, their removal from the face of the earth. But, as his friends were quick to point out, 'Bhagwan protected porcupines too,' and in any case you could never see the creatures or catch them, they were completely nocturnal.

Mr Mani got out of bed every night, torch in one hand, a stout stick in the other, but as soon as he stepped into the garden the crunching and digging stopped and he was greeted by the most infuriating of silences. He would grope around in the dark, swinging wildly with the stick, but not a single porcupine was to be seen or heard. As soon as he was back in bed—the sounds would start all over again. Scrunch, scrunch, *katar, katar...*

Mr Mani came to his class tired and dishevelled, with rings beneath his eyes and a permanent frown on his face. It took some time for his pupils to discover the reason for his misery, but when they did, they felt sorry for their teacher and took to discussing ways and means of saving his potatoes from the porcupines.

It was Prakash who came up with the idea of a moat or waterditch. 'Porcupines don't like water,' he said knowledgeably.

'How do you know?' asked one of his friends.

'Throw water on one and see how it runs! They don't like getting their quills wet.'

There was no one who could disprove Prakash's theory, and the class fell in with the idea of building a moat, especially as it meant getting most of the day off.

'Anything to make Mr Mani happy,' said the headmaster, and the rest of the school watched with envy as the pupils of Class Five, armed with spades and shovels collected from all parts of the village, took up their positions around Mr Mani's potato field and began digging a ditch.

By evening the moat was ready, but it was still dry and the porcupines got in again that night and had a great feast.

'At this rate,' said Mr Mani gloomily 'there won't be any potatoes left to save.'

But next day Prakash and the other boys and girls managed to divert the water from a stream that flowed past the village. They had the satisfaction of watching it flow gently into the ditch. Everyone went home in a good mood. By nightfall, the ditch had overflowed, the potato field was flooded, and Mr Mani found himself trapped inside his house. But Prakash and his friends had won the day. The porcupines stayed away that night!

A month had passed, and wild violets, daisies and buttercups now sprinkled the hill slopes, and on her way to school Bina gathered enough to make a little posy. The bunch of flowers fitted easily into an old ink well. Miss Ramola was delighted to find this little display in the middle of her desk.

'Who put these here?' she asked in surprise.

Bina kept quiet, and the rest of the class smiled secretively. After that, they took turns bringing flowers for the classroom.

On her long walks to school and home again, Bina became aware that April was the month of new leaves. The oak leaves were bright green above and silver beneath, and when they rippled in the breeze they were like clouds of silvery green. The path was strewn with old leaves, dry and crackly. Sonu loved kicking them around.

Clouds of white butterflies floated across the stream. Sonu was chasing a butterfly when he stumbled over something dark and repulsive. He went sprawling on the grass. When he got to his feet, he looked down at the remains of a small animal.

'Bina! Prakash! Come quickly!' he shouted.

It was part of a sheep, killed some days earlier by a much larger animal.

'Only a leopard could have done this,' said Prakash.

'Let's get away, then,' said Sonu. 'It might still be around!'

'No, there's nothing left to eat. The leopard will be hunting elsewhere by now. Perhaps it's moved on to the next valley.'

'Still, I'm frightened,' said Sonu. 'There may be more leopards!'

Bina took him by the hand. 'Leopards don't attack humans!' she said.

'They will, if they get a taste for people!' insisted Prakash.

'Well, this one hasn't attacked any people as yet,' said Bina, although she couldn't be sure. Hadn't there been rumours of a leopard attacking some workers near the dam? But she did not want Sonu to feel afraid, so she did not mention the story. All she said was, 'It has probably come here because of all the activity near the dam.'

All the same, they hurried home. And for a few days, whenever they reached the stream, they crossed over very quickly, unwilling to linger too long at that lovely spot.

5

A few days later, a school party was on its way to Tehri to see the new dam that was being built.

Miss Ramola had arranged to take her class, and Mr Mani, not wishing to be left out, insisted on taking his class as well. That meant there were about fifty boys and girls taking part in the outing. The little bus could only take thirty. A friendly truck driver agreed to take some children if they were prepared to sit on sacks of potatoes. And Prakash persuaded the owner of the diesel roller to turn it round and head it back to Tehri—with him and a couple of friends up on the driving seat.

Prakash's small group set off at sunrise, as they had to walk some distance in order to reach the stranded road roller. The bus left at 9 a.m. with Miss Ramola and her class, and Mr Mani and some of his pupils. The truck was to follow later.

It was Bina's first visit to a large town and her first bus ride.

The sharp curves along the winding, downhill road made several children feel sick. The bus driver seemed to be in a tearing hurry. He took them along at rolling, rollicking speed, which made Bina feel quite giddy. She rested her head on her arms and refused to look out of the window. Hairpin bends and cliff edges, pine forests and snowcapped peaks, all swept past her, but she felt too ill to want to look at anything. It was just as well—those sudden drops, hundreds of feet to the valley below, were quite frightening. Bina began to wish that she hadn't come—or that she had joined Prakash on the road roller instead!

Miss Ramola and Mr Mani didn't seem to notice the lurching and groaning of the old bus. They had made this journey many times. They were busy arguing about the advantages and disadvantages of large dams—an argument that was to continue on and off for much of the day; sometimes in Hindi, sometimes in English, sometimes in the local dialect!

Meanwhile, Prakash and his friends had reached the roller. The driver hadn't turned up, but they managed to reverse it and get it going in the direction of Tehri. They were soon overtaken by both the bus and the truck but kept moving along at a steady chug. Prakash spotted Bina at the window of the bus and waved cheerfully. She responded feebly.

Bina felt better when the road levelled out near Tehri. As they crossed an old bridge over the wide river, they were startled by a loud bang which made the bus shudder. A cloud of dust rose above the town.

'They're blasting the mountain,' said Miss Ramola.

'End of a mountain,' said Mr Mani mournfully.

While they were drinking cups of tea at the bus stop, waiting for the potato truck and the road roller, Miss Ramola and Mr Mani continued their argument about the dam. Miss Ramola maintained that it would bring electric power and water for irrigation to large areas of the country, including the surrounding area. Mr Mani declared that it was a menace, as it was situated in an earthquake zone. There would be a terrible disaster if the dam burst! Bina found it all very confusing. And what about the animals in the area, she wondered, what would happen to them?

The argument was becoming quite heated when the potato truck arrived. There was no sign of the road roller, so it was decided that Mr Mani should wait for Prakash and his friends while Miss Ramola's group went ahead.

Some eight or nine miles before Tehri the road roller had broken down, and Prakash and his friends were forced to walk. They had not gone far, however, when a mule train came along— five or six mules that had been delivering sacks of grain in Nauti. A boy rode on the first mule, but the others had no loads.

'Can you give us a ride to Tehri?' called Prakash.

'Make yourselves comfortable,' said the boy.

There were no saddles, only gunny sacks strapped on to the mules with rope. They had a rough but jolly ride down to the Tehri bus stop. None of them had ever ridden mules; but they had saved at least an hour on the road.

Looking around the bus stop for the rest of the party, they could find no one from their school. And Mr Mani, who should have been waiting for them, had vanished.

6

Tania Ramola and her group had taken the steep road to the hill above Tehri. Half an hour's climbing brought them to a little plateau which overlooked the town, the river and the dam site.

The earthworks for the dam were only just coming up, but a wide tunnel had been bored through the mountain to divert the river into another channel. Down below, the old town was still spread out across the valley and from a distance it looked quite charming and picturesque.

'Will the whole town be swallowed up by the waters of the dam?' asked Bina.

'Yes, all of it,' said Miss Ramola. 'The clock tower and the old palace. The long bazaar, and the temples, the schools and the jail, and hundreds of houses, for many miles up the valley. All those people will have to go—thousands of them! Of course, they'll be resettled elsewhere.'

'But the town's been here for hundreds of years,' said Bina. 'They were quite happy without the dam, weren't they?'

'I suppose they were. But the dam isn't just for them—it's for the millions who live further downstream, across the plains.'

'And it doesn't matter what happens to this place?'

'The local people will be given new homes, somewhere else.' Miss Ramola found herself on the defensive and decided to change the subject. 'Everyone must be hungry. It's time we had our lunch.'

Bina kept quiet. She didn't think the local people would want to go away. And it was a good thing, she mused, that there was only a small stream and not a big river running past her village. To be uprooted like this—a town and hundreds of villages—and put down somewhere on the hot, dusty plains—seemed to her unbearable.

'Well, I'm glad I don't live in Tehri,' she said.

She did not know it, but all the animals and most of the birds had already left the area. The leopard had been among them.

They walked through the colourful, crowded bazaar, where fruit sellers did business beside silversmiths, and pavement vendors sold everything from umbrellas to glass bangles. Sparrows attacked sacks of grain, monkeys made off with bananas, and stray cows and dogs rummaged in refuse bins, but nobody took any notice. Music blared from radios. Buses blew their horns. Sonu bought a whistle to add to the general din, but Miss Ramola told him to put it away. Bina had kept ten rupees aside, and now she used it to buy a cotton head scarf for her mother.

As they were about to enter a small restaurant for a meal, they were joined by Prakash and his companions; but of Mr Mani there was still no sign.

'He must have met one of his relatives,' said Prakash. 'He has relatives everywhere.'

After a simple meal of rice and lentils, they walked the length of the bazaar without seeing Mr Mani. At last, when they were about to give up the search, they saw him emerge from a bylane, a large sack slung over his shoulder.

'Sir, where have you been?' asked Prakash. 'We have been looking for you everywhere.'

On Mr Mani's face was a look of triumph.

'Help me with this bag,' he said breathlessly.

'You've bought more potatoes, sir,' said Prakash.

'Not potatoes, boy. Dahlia bulbs!'

## 7

It was dark by the time they were all back in Nauti. Mr Mani had refused to be separated from his sack of dahlia bulbs, and had been forced to sit in the back of the truck with Prakash and most of the boys.

Bina did not feel so ill on the return journey. Going uphill was definitely better than going downhill! But by the time the bus reached Nauti it was too late for most of the children to walk back to the more distant villages. The boys were put up in different homes, while the girls were given beds in the school verandah.

The night was warm and still. Large moths fluttered around the single bulb that lit the verandah. Counting moths, Sonu soon fell asleep. But Bina stayed awake for some time, listening to the sounds of the night. A nightjar went *tonk-tonk* in the bushes, and somewhere in the forest an owl hooted softly. The sharp call of a barking deer travelled up the valley, from the direction of the stream. Jackals kept howling. It seemed that there were more of them than ever before.

Bina was not the only one to hear the barking deer. The leopard, stretched full length on a rocky ledge, heard it too. The leopard raised its head and then got up slowly. The deer was its natural prey. But there weren't many left, and that was why the leopard, robbed of its forest by the dam, had taken to attacking dogs and cattle near the villages.

As the cry of the barking deer sounded nearer, the leopard left its lookout point and moved swiftly through the shadows towards the stream.

### 8

In early June the hills were dry and dusty, and forest fires broke out, destroying shrubs and trees, killing birds and small animals. The resin in the pines made these trees burn more fiercely, and the wind would take sparks from the trees and carry them into the dry grass and leaves, so that new fires would spring up before the old ones had died out. Fortunately, Bina's village was not in the pine belt; the fires did not reach it. But Nauti was surrounded by a fire that raged for three days, and the children had to stay away from school.

And then, towards the end of June, the monsoon rains arrived and there was an end to forest fires. The monsoon lasts three months and the lower Himalayas would be drenched in rain, mist and cloud for the next three months.

The first rain arrived while Bina, Prakash and Sonu were returning home from school. Those first few drops on the dusty path made them cry out with excitement. Then the rain grew heavier and a wonderful aroma rose from the earth.

'The best smell in the world!' exclaimed Bina.

Everything suddenly came to life. The grass, the crops, the trees, the birds. Even the leaves of the trees glistened and looked new.

That first wet weekend, Bina and Sonu helped their mother plant beans, maize and cucumbers. Sometimes, when the rain was very heavy, they had to run indoors. Otherwise they worked in the rain, the soft mud clinging to their bare legs.

Prakash now owned a black dog with one ear up and one ear down. The dog ran around getting in everyone's way, barking at cows, goats, hens and humans, without frightening any of them. Prakash said it was a very clever dog, but no one else seemed to think so. Prakash also said it would protect the village from the leopard, but others said the dog would be the first to be taken—he'd run straight into the jaws of Mr Spots!

In Nauti, Tania Ramola was trying to find a dry spot in the quarters she'd been given. It was an old building and the roof was leaking in several places. Mugs and buckets were scattered about the floor in order to catch the drip.

Mr Mani had dug up all his potatoes and presented them to the friends and neighbours who had given him lunches and dinners. He was having the time of his life, planting dahlia bulbs all over his garden.

'I'll have a field of many-coloured dahlias!' he announced. 'Just wait till the end of August!'

'Watch out for those porcupines,' warned his sister. 'They eat dahlia bulbs too!'

Mr Mani made an inspection tour of his moat, no longer in flood, and found everything in good order. Prakash had done his job well.

Now, when the children crossed the stream, they found that the water level had risen by about a foot. Small cascades had turned into waterfalls. Ferns had sprung up on the banks. Frogs chanted.

Prakash and his dog dashed across the stream. Bina and Sonu followed more cautiously. The current was much stronger now and the water was almost up to their knees. Once they had crossed the stream, they hurried along the path, anxious not to be caught in a sudden downpour.

By the time they reached school, each of them had two or three leeches clinging to their legs. They had to use salt to remove them. The leeches were the most troublesome part of the rainy season. Even the leopard did not like them. It could not lie in the long grass without getting leeches on its paws and face.

One day, when Bina, Prakash and Sonu were about to cross the stream they heard a low rumble, which grew louder every second. Looking up at the opposite hill, they saw several trees shudder, tilt outwards and begin to fall. Earth and rocks bulged out from the mountain, then came crashing down into the ravine.

'Landslide!' shouted Sonu.

'It's carried away the path,' said Bina. 'Don't go any further.'

There was a tremendous roar as more rocks, trees and bushes fell away and crashed down the hillside.

Prakash's dog, who had gone ahead, came running back, tail between his legs.

They remained rooted to the spot until the rocks had stopped falling and the dust had settled. Birds circled the area, calling wildly. A frightened barking deer ran past them.

'We can't go to school now,' said Prakash. 'There's no way

around.'

They turned and trudged home through the gathering mist.

In Koli, Prakash's parents had heard the roar of the landslide. They were setting out in search of the children when they saw them emerge from the mist, waving cheerfully.

### 9

They had to miss school for another three days, and Bina was afraid they might not be able to take their final exams. Although Prakash was not really troubled at the thought of missing exams, he did not like feeling helpless just because their path had been swept away. So he explored the hillside until he found a goat track going around the mountain. It joined up with another path near Nauti. This made their walk longer by a mile, but Bina did not mind. It was much cooler now that the rains were in full swing.

The only trouble with the new route was that it passed close to the leopard's lair. The animal had made this area its own since being forced to leave the dam area.

One day Prakash's dog ran ahead of them, barking furiously. Then he ran back, whimpering.

'He's always running away from something,' observed Sonu. But a minute later he understood the reason for the dog's fear.

They rounded a bend and Sonu saw the leopard standing in their way. They were struck dumb—too terrified to run. It was a strong, sinewy creature. A low growl rose from its throat. It seemed ready to spring.

They stood perfectly still, afraid to move or say a word. And the leopard must have been equally surprised. It stared at them for a few seconds, then bounded across the path and into the oak forest.

Sonu was shaking. Bina could hear her heart hammering. Prakash could only stammer: 'Did you see the way he sprang? Wasn't he beautiful?'

He forgot to look at his watch for the rest of the day.

A few days later Sonu stopped and pointed to a large outcrop of rock on the next hill.

The leopard stood far above them, outlined against the sky. It looked strong, majestic. Standing beside it were two young cubs.

'Look at those little ones!' exclaimed Sonu.

'So it's a female, not a male,' said Prakash.

'That's why she was killing so often,' said Bina. 'She had to feed her cubs too.'

They remained still for several minutes, gazing up at the leopard and her cubs. The leopard family took no notice of them.

'She knows we are here,' said Prakash, 'but she doesn't care. She knows we won't harm them.'

'We are cubs too!' said Sonu.

'Yes,' said Bina. 'And there's still plenty of space for all of us. Even when the dam is ready there will still be room for leopards and humans.'

## 10

The school exams were over. The rains were nearly over too. The landslide had been cleared, and Bina, Prakash and Sonu were once again crossing the stream.

There was a chill in the air, for it was the end of September.

Prakash had learnt to play the flute quite well, and he played on the way to school and then again on the way home. As a result he did not look at his watch so often.

One morning they found a small crowd in front of Mr Mani's house.

'What could have happened?' wondered Bina. 'I hope he hasn't got lost again.'

'Maybe he's sick,' said Sonu.

'Maybe it's the porcupines,' said Prakash.

But it was none of these things.

Mr Mani's first dahlia was in bloom, and half the village had turned out to look at it! It was a huge red double dahlia, so heavy that it had to be supported with sticks. No one had ever seen such a magnificent flower!

Mr Mani was a happy man. And his mood only improved over the coming week, as more and more dahlias flowered—crimson, yellow, purple, mauve, white—button dahlias, pompom dahlias, spotted dahlias, striped dahlias... Mr Mani had them all! A dahlia even turned up on Tania Romola's desk—he got on quite well with her now—and another brightened up the headmaster's study.

A week later, on their way home—it was almost the last day of the school term—Bina, Prakash and Sonu talked about what they might do when they grew up.

'I think I'll become a teacher,' said Bina. 'I'll teach children about animals and birds, and trees and flowers.'

'Better than maths!' said Prakash.

'I'll be a pilot,' said Sonu. 'I want to fly a plane like Miss Ramola's brother.'

'And what about you, Prakash?' asked Bina.

Prakash just smiled and said, 'Maybe I'll be a flute player,' and he put the flute to he lips and played a sweet melody.

'Well, the world needs flute players too,' said Bina, as they fell into step beside him.

The leopard had been stalking a barking deer. She paused when she heard the flute and the voices of the children. Her own young ones were growing quickly, but the girl and the two boys did not look much older.

They had started singing their favourite song again.

> *Five more miles to go!*
> *We climb through rain and snow.*
> *A river to cross...*
> *A mountain to pass...*
> *Now we've four more miles to go!*

The leopard waited until they had passed, before returning to the trail of the barking deer.

# White Clouds, Green Mountains

Towards the end of September, those few monsoon clouds that still linger over the Himalayas are no longer burdened with rain and are able to assume unusual shapes and patterns, chasing each other across the sky and disappearing in spectacular sunset formations.

I have always found this to be the best time of the year in the hills. The sun-drenched hillsides are still an emerald green; the air is crisp, but winter's bite is still a month or two away; and for those who still like to take to the open road on foot, there are springs, streams and waterfalls tumbling over rocks that remain dry for most of the year. The lizard that basked on a sun-baked slab of granite last May is missing, but in his place the spotted forktail trips daintily among the boulders in a stream; and the strident sound of the cicadas is gradually replaced by the gentler trilling of the crickets and grasshoppers.

Cicadas, as you probably know, make their music with their legs, which are moved like the bows of violins against their bodies. It's rather like an orchestra tuning up but never quite getting on with the overture or symphony. Aunt Ruby, who is a little deaf, can nevertheless hear the cicadas when they are at their loudest. She lives not far from a large boarding-school, and one day when I remarked that I could hear the school choir or choral group singing, she nodded and remarked: 'Yes, dear. They do it with their legs, don't they?'

Come to think of it, that school choir does sound a bit squeaky.

Now, more than at any other time of the year, the wildflowers come into their own.

The hillside is covered with a sward of flowers and ferns. Sprays of wild ginger, tangles of clematis, flat clusters of yarrow and lady's mantle. The datura grows everywhere with its graceful white balls and prickly fruits. And the wild woodbine provides the stems from which the village boys make their flutes.

Aroids are plentiful and attract attention by their resemblance to snakes with protruding tongues—hence the popular name, cobra lily. This serpent's tongue is a perfect landing-stage for flies etc., who, crawling over the male flowers in their eager search for the liquor that lies at the base of the spike (a liquor that is most appealing to their depraved appetites), succeed in fertilising the female flowers as they proceed. We see that it is not only humans who become addicted to alcohol. Bears have been known to get drunk on the juice of rhododendron flowers, while bumble bees can be out-and-out dipsomaniacs.

One of the more spectacular cobra lilies, which rejoices in the name *Sauromotum Guttatum*—ask your nearest botanist what that means!—bears a solitary leaf and purple spathe. When the seeds form, it withdraws the spike underground; and when the rains are over and the soil is not too damp, it sends it up again covered with scarlet berries. In the opinion of the hill folk, the appearance of the red spike is more to be relied on as a forecast of the end of the monsoon than any meteorological expertise. Up here on the ranges that fall between the Jumna and the Bhagirathi (known as the Rawain), we can be perfectly sure of fine weather a fortnight after the fiery spike appears.

But it is the commelina, more than any other Himalayan flower, that takes my breath away. The secret is in its colour—a pure pristine blue that seems to reflect the deepest blue of the sky. Towards the end of the rains it appears as if from nowhere, graces the hillside for the space of about two weeks, and disappears again until the following monsoon.

When I see the first commelina, I stand dumb before it and the world stands still while I worship. So absorbed do I become in its delicate beauty that I begin to doubt the reality of everything else in the world.

But only for a moment. The blare of a truck's horn reminds me that I am still lingering on the main road leading out of the hill station. A cloud of dust and blasts of diesel fumes are further indications that reality takes many different forms, assailing all my senses at once! Even my commelina seems to shrink from the onslaught. But as it is still there, I take heart and leave the highway for a lesser road.

Soon I have left the clutter of the town behind. What did Aunt Ruby say the other day? 'Stand still for five minutes, and they will build a hotel on top of you.'

Wasn't it Lot's wife who was turned into a pillar of salt

when she looked back at the doomed city that had been her home? I have an uneasy feeling that I will be turned into a pillar of cement if I look back, so I plod on along the road to Devsari, a kindly village in the valley. It will be some time before 'developers' and big money boys get here, for no one will go to live where there is no driveway!

A tea-shop beckons. How would one manage in the hills without these wayside tea-shops? Miniature inns, they provide food, shelter, and even lodging to dozens at a time.

I tackle some buns that have a pre-Independence look about them. They are rock-hard, to match the environment, but I manage to swallow some of the jagged pieces with the hot sweet tea, which is good.

www.ingramcontent.com/pod-product-compliance
Lightning Source LLC
Chambersburg PA
CBHW031517270326
41930CB00006B/427